To
Allyson—
Bookof
&
Go Lady Ote

[signature]

SPORT IS LIFE
with the Volume Turned Up

JOAN CRONAN

with Rob Schriver

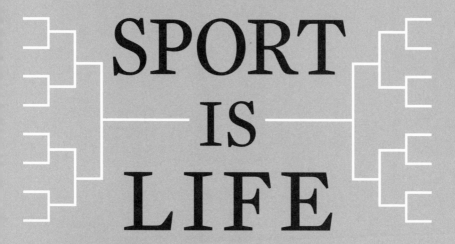

SPORT IS LIFE

with the Volume Turned Up

Lessons Learned
that Apply to Business and Life

THE UNIVERSITY OF TENNESSEE PRESS
Knoxville

Copyright © 2015 by The University of Tennessee Press /
Knoxville.

All Rights Reserved. Manufactured in the
United States of America.

Cloth: 1st printing, 2015; 2nd printing, 2016.

The paper in this book meets the requirements of American
National Standards Institute / National Information Standards
Organization specification Z39.48–1992 (Permanence of Paper).
It contains 30 percent post-consumer waste and is certified by
the Forest Stewardship Council.

Library of Congress Cataloging-in-Publication Data
Cronan, Joan.
Sport is life with the volume turned up : lessons learned that
apply to business and life / Joan Cronan with Rob Schriver. —
First Edition.
      pages cm
  Includes bibliographical references.
  ISBN 978-1-62190-212-6 (Hardcover : alk. paper)
  1. Cronan, Joan.
  2. Athletic directors—United States—Biography.
  3. Conduct of life. I. Title.

GV697.C76A3 2015
796.01—dc23
                          2015024895

Tom—my inspiration
Kristi and Stacey—my pride, my loves, and my legacy
Kent and Rhett—the two best sons-in-law ever
Chase, Reed, Quinn, Reese, and Larkin—my joy
Coaches, staff, and business partners—my support
Family and friends—my foundation
Todd Greene—my advisor and coach
Rob Schriver—my coauthor, colleague, and friend

—Joan Cronan

To Debby, Kate, and Julia.

—Rob Schriver

CONTENTS

PAT SUMMITT

(June 14, 1952 – June 28, 2016)

Dedicated to the memory of Pat Summitt
whose stunning accomplishments were matched
only by her deep humility and her passion
to make a difference
for others through athletics.

FOREWORD

Lady Vol Head Coach Pat Summitt built the
women's basketball program at the University
of Tennessee, coaching thirty-eight years. Before
she retired in 2012, her teams won sixteen SEC
titles, went to eighteen Final Fours, and won
eight national titles. Most importantly, her student
athletes who played all four years achieved a
100% graduation rate.

Dear Readers,

Joan Cronan's leadership qualities were key to growing
support and loyalty for all Lady Vol sports. Her competitive nature fueled us all to be the best.

Joan's vision, passion, and tireless efforts to grow
women's athletics and to promote women's opportunities have made a huge difference across the nation for
women in sports. Joan was a driving force in elevating the
prominence and brand of Tennessee Lady Vol athletics
through strategy, excellence, and priceless relationships.
Some of Joan's greatest strengths are leadership, development, business, and marketing skills.

Joan expected my best each day, and I expected her best each day. Over the years, Joan and I sharpened each other. I consider her a great friend and true champion.

Joan builds lasting relationships in her career. I am thankful to be one of them. I am so glad she came to Tennessee and led our UT women's athletic programs. I think we made a GREAT TEAM!!

Pat Summitt

FOREWORD

Sally Jenkins has been a staff writer for the *Washington Post* since 2000. Four of the twelve books she has authored have been *New York Times* best sellers, the most recent of which is *Sum It Up*, which features legendary Lady Vol Basketball Coach Pat Summitt. A Texas native, Sally graduated from Stanford University and lives in Sag Harbor, New York.

Joan and Pat Summitt were what I call "glass cutters" in building the Tennessee women's athletics program. They did not break the glass ceiling; they carefully carved their way through.

Joan was a revolutionary in a way people found acceptable. She befriended prominent leaders in sports and business to overcome resistance to women's sports at a football school in the South.

As an observer of UT women's sports since 1997, I have been fascinated at how Joan successfully persuaded people to invest in the Lady Vol program.

Some dynasties have a protective environment. But that was not the case at Tennessee. They were fun to be around. Interesting and fun . . . and there was an openness.

Joan is a great diplomat. I've observed her in action. She can juggle a lot of elements. And *everyone* likes and respects her. That's not always the case with the person in charge.

Sally Jenkins

ACKNOWLEDGMENTS

Special thanks for editing to:
Lynne McCombs
Debby Schriver
Anne M. McKinney
The Rev. David and Jan Luckett
Mike Levesque
Todd Greene
Merrily Baker
Trudy Reeves

And, thanks to our book team at UT Press:
Scot Danforth
Kelly Gray
Emily Huckabay
Kathryn Peck
Tom Post

PURPOSE

Not many people have an opportunity to live their dream. Since I was twelve years old, my dream has been to provide opportunities for women to learn to compete and succeed.

Denied the opportunity to play Little League baseball with the boys hurt. Yet, it became a defining moment in my life: I set a goal that this would not happen to other young women, and that goal became my passion. This book is about the paths I followed from that day forward to help ensure equal opportunities for all. Now, looking back, I can pinpoint the specific time and event in my life that motivated me toward my goals. That day I discovered that I did not want to be a spectator. I did not want to collect the bats after the game. I did not want to keep stats.

I WANTED TO PLAY.

This book includes peaks and valleys, strategies and stories, laughs and tears. But I can assure you as I sit and watch women compete at the highest level whether on television, in person, in the Olympics, and in high school, college, or pro, I am proud I was a part of this success. I surrounded myself with great people and a University that supported women.

RING THE BELLS
—EVERY DAY

Leading one of the top women's sports programs in the country taught me many lessons about life and business. I have tried to use lessons from the world of athletics to help individuals and organizations reach higher performance levels, too.

Of all the things we do in life, keeping our priorities straight is one of the most important. If you were to ask me what my priorities are, I would immediately say God, family, friends, the University of Tennessee, the state of Tennessee, the city of Knoxville, golf, tennis, etc. But then, if you asked me whether I always keep them in order, I would have to say no. So, knowing prioritizing is a challenge, I came up with a system that has helped me.

I like to make lists and check things off of them. I have even been known to add something after I have done it, just so I can check it off. I came up with B-E-L-L-S as a "to do" acronym. Every day I try to ring the bells.

B—Bible
E—Exercise
L—Letter
L—Learn
S—Special Project

We all wish we could ring them every day, but we shouldn't beat ourselves up if we don't. It's a goal. "Ringing the BELLS" includes the following five steps:

B—I begin each day by reading my Bible or a Bible devotional. This starts my day off right. One of my favorite devotional books is *Jesus Calling* by Sarah Young.

E—I try to do something physical (exercise) that is good for my body. That then empowers me to do more physical activities: golf, walking, tennis . . .

L—I write a letter of encouragement to someone I care about—not one I *have* to write, but one I *want* to write. IMPORTANT: It has to be a handwritten note. Emails don't count. I treasure the handwritten notes from former coaches and student athletes who talk about how our program made a difference for them.

L—I try to learn something new every day. For example, I am a huge fan of Words with Friends (an online game of Scrabble). And my learning could be as simple as discovering a new word.

Lady Vol Coach Pat Summitt provided me with a good lesson here. In 2007 Coach Summitt's team lost in a regional NCAA final game to Xavier University. After the game, something happened that I did not expect. Pat came to me and said that it was her fault they lost the game. Xavier had used what is called the Princeton offense, and she didn't understand it enough to defend it. Coach wanted to bring in a specialist on that offense in order to learn it. She said that she did not want this type of loss to happen again. So, here is a basketball coach, considered by many to be the best in America, wanting more information so that she can learn something new that will help her to be better at her job in the future. Isn't that something?

S—Special project. I have always been able to keep life organized better at the office than at home. I hate housework. Therefore, for me, my special project is doing something around the house. It could be as exciting as cleaning out the vegetable drawer or straightening my sock drawer. Eventually, the house is organized. It is like eating that elephant: you just keep taking one bite at a time.

Yes, I hate housework, so much so that when my son-in-law Rhett recently took a job as an executive with Electrolux, my first comments to him were, "Congratulations, but don't send me any vacuum cleaners. I have lived 70 years without a vacuum cleaner that fit in my hands. So, I don't want one now. But it's okay for you to send me some of those high-end Electrolux kitchen appliances."

I wish I could tell you I make the BELLS ring every day, but I don't. On the days I do, though, I feel a lot better.

My challenge to you is to come up with a system that works best for you.

Kathy Wuethrich, a friend of my daughter Stacey's, recently called and asked if she could amend the BELLS system to become BELTS. As a busy young mother she would like to text rather than write letters. And I do believe that we all have seasons in our lives that are busier than others, so I gave her special dispensation—for a limited time only.

INTRODUCTION

Sometimes sports and business (and life) look like a roller coaster. There are peaks and valleys; ups and downs; wins and losses; good years and off years. How can you and your life's work become more consistent—more reliable? How do you maintain steady growth year after year? Is it luck? Is it skill?

I've often found that the harder I work, the luckier I get.

I think the model for personal and professional growth is a gradual, sustained growth over a period of time. I also think it ties to the core notion presented in these writings: assemble a solid team of people, then grow their skills, and in turn, their pride. And create a climate where passion emerges and enhances team performance and success. This is not a dream—unless, you say it was my dream in building a sustained success with the University of Tennessee women's athletics program over a thirty-year period.

According to Napoleon Hill, a goal is a dream with a deadline. It's not enough to say you want to recruit the three best players in the country. You have to say who they are and decide when and how you will recruit them. Then you have to do it.

My thoughts in this book are organized into four fundamental topics.

People
Pride
Passion
Persistence

The first is *people*. Okay, that's simple. It's the beginning. I worked in a people business; you do, too. I challenge you to name a business or organization that isn't all about people.

Legendary basketball Coach John Wooden from UCLA used a model he called "pyramid for success." Wooden said that friendship, loyalty, and cooperation build a solid base for success, then skills and team spirit come together at the next level, and finally, competitive greatness is reached at the pinnacle[1]—not unlike the UT Lady Vols in our early stages. It's like you and your organization coming together today—your talented people with a cause or mission, and a good idea.

So, that is the start—part one—phase one. In the people stage, we will discuss building trust, delegating tasks to others, and even saying thank you along the way.

But what's next? What is the next phase or building block for us? It is pride! Pride is beyond just belonging; it is higher self-esteem. Pride is being more independent.[2] According to football coaching legend Vince Lombardi, "Confidence is contagious. So is lack of confidence."[3]

Pride. People developing pride. Proud people accomplishing tasks, reaching their goals, changing the way they see themselves. Developing new processes and strategies. Taking their work to another level.

So, we come together. We form teams and work relationships in the first level. Then we move to more independence and higher self-esteem—pride—in ourselves in the second level. Good people adding pride to their toolbox. And this strengthening of self also contributes to a strengthening of the team.

Finally, we progress to the third phase: passion. In the passion phase, the individual is performing at a high level, and the team is performing at a higher level. The team may become more interdependent now, and as a result, your game plan begins to work. We have all seen athletic teams that are in the "zone." And as an example, a great defensive basketball team coming together can take a strong offensive team right out of their game.

In his successful book *Good to Great,* Jim Collins says that passion is an integral part of business strategy. He explains, "You can't manufacture passion or motivate people to feel passionate. You can only discover what ignites your passion and the passions of those around you."[4]

This passion puts your team in the zone. This is a plan coming together—as the "A-Team" used to say. This is doing what you love to do, what you do best, what you were trained to do. This is you and your organization at your best. For example, this could be when people pay you or your organization a compliment.

Persistence is just that—an endurance, a drive, and even a doggedness to succeed. This section includes a few more quick hits to help us win the game.

ESPN wanted to interview me a few years ago. They wanted me to tell them the keys to our success with the University of Tennessee Lady Vols. I was ready to give them at least a thirty-minute speech, but they wanted only a short sound bite. I simply said, "The Lady Vols have developed a pride, a passion, and a persistence, and these have become keys to our success."

This book is my opportunity to provide more than a short sound bite or even a thirty-minute speech. In part 1, I'll get into the principles of finding the right people. In part 2, I'll show you how to help the right people develop pride. In part 3, I'll describe how to develop that pride into a passion that will transform your organization and set your goals sky high. I have said that I think the key to success in athletics is the right people developing a pride and a passion, and you know, it's the same way in your life and in your business. Motivational and business books remind and encourage you to do the right thing, but I hope this book takes it one step further for you: I hope it helps you in your journey toward the championship you want to win.

So:

PEOPLE > PRIDE > PASSION > PERSISTENCE.

ABOUT ME

I believe that it is important to have dreams and goals. As a twelve-year-old, I was upset because I was not allowed to play Little League baseball. Fast forward to the summer of 2014, and a twelve-year-old girl pitched in the Little League World Series, she threw the first pitch out to start a 2014 World Series game between the Giants and the Royals, and she even had her picture on the cover of *Sports Illustrated*.

As for me, however, I *was* the starting guard for the Opelousas High School basketball team as a freshman, and we won the district championship that year. Maybe I shouldn't go that far back, but I am very proud of that accomplishment. I had a great coach and motivated teammates. Yet even after a successful high school career, I had very few opportunities as a young woman to compete at a higher level.

It has been my goal to establish and keep the University of Tennessee as one of the premier women's athletic departments in the nation and to improve women's opportunities in athletics as a whole. I am very proud of the fact that UT either captured the Southeastern Conference's Women's All-Sport Award or finished second as recognized by the *New York Times* for five out of seven years during my tenure.

In 2014, the *Sports Business Journal* recognized me as one of their Champions in Sports Business; this was a great honor. It was also a privilege to serve as president of both the National Association of Collegiate Women Athletics Administrators (NACWAA) and the National Association of Collegiate Directors of Athletics (NACDA), and also to be recognized by these groups as one of the Athletic Directors of the Year. Being recognized by your peers is an honor, and I am particularly proud of these awards.

You may not know that I came to the University of Tennessee from the College of Charleston, where I was athletics director for ten years and later inducted into the "C of C" Hall of Fame. In 1980, the American Women's Sports Foundation recognized the school as having the number-one women's athletics program in the country—quite an honor for us!

Outside the University of Tennessee, I have served as president of the TN Sports Hall of Fame and on the boards of First Tennessee Bank, Leadership Knoxville (of which I am chair), the U.S. Sports Academy, East Tennessee Children's Hospital, Baptist Hospital, and the YMCA. I am in the Tennessee Sports Hall of Fame, the LSU Hall of Distinction, and the Knoxville Sports Hall of Fame; the Fellowship of Christian Athletes, which is an important organization to me, has also placed me in their Hall of Champions. I am involved in Athletes in Action, and I am a deacon at Central Baptist Church in Knoxville's Bearden community. Other leadership roles of mine over the years have included chairing the 1991 Knoxville area United

Way Fund Drive and serving as president of the Executive Women's Association. These have all been amazing experiences.

In addition to serving in these different capacities over the years, my hard work has earned me awards in both leadership and communication. In 1987 the Women's Basketball Coaches Association honored my work by presenting me with its leadership award—it was also an opportunity to serve on both the SEC's and NCAA's Executive Committee. Seven years later, in 1994, I received the Toastmaster's International Communication and Leadership Award and also earned the Alpha Omicron Pi Citizen of the Year Award. In 2014 the YWCA selected me as one of thirty women who made a difference in Knoxville over the past thirty years, and most recently, the new Lady Vol Volleyball Practice Center was named in my honor, as well as the street that leads to the Center, which is now called Joan Cronan Way—something that makes me extremely proud! There is a newly endowed Joan Cronan Sports Management Fellowship that will provide scholarships for former Lady Vols who want to pursue a career in athletic administration, too.

I am now spending a lot of my time working on development for the Pat Summitt Foundation as well as being a founding partner of a business consulting group—DIREC Consulting. The consulting group specializes in teamwork, leadership, and creating a winning attitude. Thus, we strive to help good companies become great. I also will continue to be a motivational speaker working with organizations and corporations.

These leadership awards have been so gratifying, but when asked what I am most proud of, I answer without hesitation that it is my involvement with people. Being a good wife, being a good mother, and being a good friend are all very important. It is where I have put a lot of my energy. Let's talk more about my philosophy of leadership as we go along.

SPORT IS LIFE
with the Volume Turned Up

1

PEOPLE

According to the *Portland Business Journal*, people skills are:

> —Understanding ourselves and moderating our responses,
>
> —Talking effectively and accurately, and
>
> —Building relationships and productive interactions.[5]

1) Understanding ourselves, 2) empathizing, 3) building trust—whew!—none of these are easy; none of these three skills are for beginners. They require work and life experience. For me, and for you, too, probably the most important ingredient needed to accomplish this is an awareness of the importance of people in your life! Barbara Streisand said it pretty well in her song: "People who need people are the luckiest people in the world."

"People skills" include both psychological and social factors. Guidelines relating to what recent generations called "people skills" have been recorded from early times. Two examples appeared in the Old Testament: Leviticus 19:18 says, "Do not seek revenge or bear a grudge against your people, but love your neighbor as yourself," while the Book of Proverbs 15:1 states, "A gentle answer turns away wrath, but a harsh word stirs up anger."

Human relations studies became more of a movement in the early 1900s as companies became more interested in the interpersonal skills of their employees. In organizations, improving people skills became a role of the corporate trainer and often a training venture. Later, in 1936, American writer Dale Carnegie popularized people skills in his book *How to Win Friends and Influence People.*[6]

People skills are important; there is no doubt. In my experience, they are huge (Goleman 1996).[7] Early success for me was making good grades in school, but I also realized that there was a broader element that was a key to success. It was in motivating others, seeing how others reacted to situations, and then handling interpersonal relationships—the people part.

I have noticed that interpersonal or social skills may be even more important at higher levels in a given organization—at the managerial level. I believe that senior managers must be tuned into this skill set. Employees are often promoted because of their technical skills, but in reality people skills become their stumbling block. We need to spend as much time working on leadership and personal effectiveness skills as we do working on technical skills.

I think head coaches have a responsibility to their assistants to emphasize their accountability in this area—in leadership and interpersonal skills. We often see coaches who are outstanding assistant coaches, but when they are promoted just one chair down to the head coaching position, they fail. It's only eighteen inches, but it's a long way. They do not fail because of their understanding of the game; they fail because they lack leadership and interpersonal skills.

The most important thing you will do is select the people with whom you surround yourself. There is something that stands out about people with more awareness of themselves and their social context; they are often more successful with interactions and relationships. It is interesting to me that women outscore men in self-management, social awareness, and relationship management.[8]

You win with people.

If you want to succeed, reach out.
—"Word for You Today,"
Bob Gass Ministries

By love serve one another.
—Galatians 5:13

NETWORKING

I believe that you won't succeed in life unless you are well connected—and that is something you have to work on. And those who enable you to succeed don't always come to you. Usually, you have to go to them.

This has been a big deal in my career and in my life.

I think it can be a key to your success.

Success, however, won't always come knocking on your door; you have to go find it. Success won't come to you. Take it to the streets if you will—good sales reps know that they must get out of the office to make sales.

There are two kinds of people in your life:

1. Those who already know you have something they need, and

2. Those who don't know it yet.

What's keeping you from reaching out? Could it be fear of rejection? Until your dream becomes more important than your fear of rejection, you may not succeed. Remember, even successful people fear rejection; the difference is they believe their goals are worth the risk.

The law of relationships says every person is only four people away from the person he or she needs. This means you know Bill, who knows Judy, who knows Charles, who knows the person you want to meet. You are already networked, aren't you? Follow the connections and you'll get to your goal.

We have all heard the saying, "It's not what you know; it's who you know." More importantly, it's not what you know, and it's not who you know; it is WHO KNOWS YOU. Take the time to let people know you. For me, the key is making networking a part of the work that I do. Also, what if you could truly think of networking as reaching out—as a task that could help others, too? If it leads to a benefit for you, that's great; if not, it benefits others and the world.

In his "Passive Panda" Newsletter on networking tips, renowned entrepreneur James Clear asks: What if you reached out to just one person each day?[9] It only takes a few minutes for each contact. That would be roughly five people per week, then roughly two hundred and fifty per year. It is important to note, though, that I have always felt it isn't necessary to have a huge cadre of acquaintances. I try to focus on people who are really important to me. If I have a strong link with ten people, that seems better than a long list of mere contacts.

Also, I never wanted to network only with people in my area of business—sports administration. I wanted to reach beyond the sports world of work to learn and gain from best practices in other areas. I had to catch myself at times. I did not want to overlook someone who I could learn from or work with for our mutual success. Sometimes this reaching out may link you up with a contact you will really need in the future.

One last thought: pick up the phone or get face-to-face. It is so much stronger to hear a voice or see the facial expressions. I think this is important. One of my favorite songs is "Reach Out and Touch Someone"—the old AT&T jingle. It is more important to talk with someone than to just email or text.

Thirty years ago, not too long after I came back to UT and Knoxville, I was invited to be part of the first Leadership Knoxville Program. This was a great opportunity for me to build a network. As vice-chair for many years and now chair of this program, I realize Leadership Knoxville has been an integral part of my network—and it continues to be a strong networking group for me.

Starting to network is important, but staying in touch with people could be even more important. I love and enjoy my friends and colleagues. In fact, I have many groups of friends—my South Carolina tennis pals, my "Yah Yah" sisters (high school friends), my Citadel friends, my movie club, my traveling friends, my golf group, and my Sunday school class. One of my goals now is to learn to play bridge, and then I will have a group of bridge friends. I love staying connected.

Success always begins somewhere, at some moment, with someone. But you have to reach out to others and make it happen.

Okay, one more networking view: I am on life support.

Networking is my life support system. I do not have any tubes or wires plugged into me. I am not hooked into a machine. But my life does depend on the system that has helped me to thrive. I bet you have one, too. If not, this may be something for you to work on. Who provides your life support?

Fortunately for me, there are many. People like my daughters, Kristi and Stacey; Coach Pat Summitt; my high school basketball coach, Anne Hollier; former Lady Vol basketball players, Jane Fleming and Anne Sprouse; philanthropist, Sherri Lee; Ann Furrow, the first female to receive an athletic scholarship at the University of Tennessee; Susan Williams, former Director of Development and UT Board of Trustees member; Carol Evans, former Director of Marketing and now Executive Director of Legacy Parks Foundation; Founder and CEO of Bandit Lights, Mike Strickland; Jimmy Cheek, Chancellor of the University of Tennessee; Dr. Mike McIntyre, UT Business School Professor; business leaders, Jim Haslam, Sam Furrow, Doug White, Brenda Lawson, Pete Claussen, Wayne Basler, and Patricia Bible; Dr. Bob Kaplan, a leading dermatologist; my friends and advisors, Elaine and Jan Williams, Margaret and Hank Dye, and Betsy Roberts; and also, important mentors to me over the years, Dr. Bill Emendorfer, Executive Director of the Tennessee Sports Hall of Fame, and Lynn Johnson, a retired executive from the Eastman Company.

My life support system has been a key to my success in athletic administration, my effectiveness in business, and my happiness in life. When I am able to build a strong working or professional relationship, I find that it is really important to maintain that relationship. I want my connections to be genuine, lasting, two-way-street bonds.

A lie puts all past truth in doubt.
—Anonymous

TRUST

How do you build trust? Many think it does not happen quickly. But what about a situation where you encounter a new business acquaintance? What about a first encounter with a recruit, coach, supplier, or work associate? What about situations where you need to build trust fast—right when you meet?

How can you assure someone you have their best interest in mind, even if they don't know you very well? How can you connect with them in a very short amount of time?

Is it possible?

I think it is.

Here's what I suggest:

The first thing you must do to build trust is always tell the truth. The second is to do what you say you are going to do (more on this later).

Smile. Have open, receptive body language. Use a calming tone of voice. These factors are very important. They are very important to help put someone else at ease. I've got to get people to talk with me and be honest with me!

Along the way, good communications skills and approachability make this happen.

This may be the key to connecting with the other person. You can do it. Oh, and by the way, once they open up, make sure to listen to what they have to say. But that is another section. (I'm getting ahead of myself.)

Trust is the foundation of communication and problem solving. It is fundamental. If I do not establish trust, what hope do I have of communicating, working effectively, and/or solving problems?

Let me tell you a story about building trust. I was in Nashville recently speaking to the Nashville Women's Club. The person who introduced me said to the group, "I do not know what Joan is going to talk about at our meeting today, but I know that afterwards she will be your best friend." I took that as the ultimate compliment; I was able to "connect" with the group. I was able to earn their trust, and I felt good about connecting with them, too.

I can also think about a time when I did not connect. I was giving a talk to a group about trying to merge two organizations. And I used an example of building a successful basketball team with the emphasis on the importance of the role of the point guard pulling a team together. In conclusion, I thought I had done a good job, until a person asked me, "What's a point guard?" I did not connect.

I can remember a time when near the end of a basketball game, Pat called for a timeout. She designed a play for one particular player to take the last shot. As the huddle was about to break, another player said, "I don't think she really wants the ball, but I do." The coaches and team had to trust each other in that instant to make a change. It took guts to speak up, and it took trust to make the change. Guess what? It worked. And we won.

What do you think? How important is trust? You know, in my next edition of this book, I may just put this on page one. It certainly is a good place to begin.

Surround yourself with the best people
you can find. Delegate authority.
And don't interfere as long as the policy
you decided on is being carried out.
—Ronald Reagan

You can delegate authority but
you can't delegate responsibility.
—Byron Dorgan

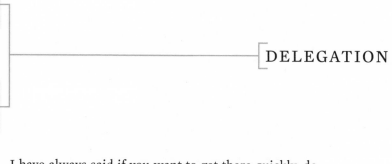

DELEGATION

I have always said if you want to get there quickly, do it yourself. If you want to go further, do it together. According to well-known financial executive Robert Pozen, "The way you delegate is that first you have to hire people who you really have confidence in. You won't truly let those people feel a sense of autonomy if you don't have confidence in them."

In a recent meeting I had with a young employee, she complained that while she was interested in more responsible work and taking on new challenges, she felt that her manager was just giving her more work to do.

Period. Some of the delegated work was challenging; yet she believed her manager didn't understand the difference. She spent a great deal of her time doing work of a repetitive nature. This workload interfered with her ability to take on more responsibility.

So I suggested that her manager balance the delegation of more work with the delegation of work requiring more responsibility. Consider again Robert Pozen's comment above. There are two key points that ring true for me:

1. Recruit and hire the right people. Develop a team. Again, it's very important in both sports and business.

2. Make sure your people are playing in the right positions.

I had a chance to hire a new staff member who would work directly with me. There were two final candidates who were very qualified and whom I really liked. One was like me. The other was the opposite of me. I chose the one not like me. I think it was a good choice; this person added another dimension to my team and my thinking. I was also better able to delegate to her, because she could do things that I could not. Her approach complemented my skills and made us a stronger department.

It's the same thing with a basketball team. What if you are looking for a point guard? (The point guard brings the ball up the court and usually calls the plays. See the section on Trust on page 13 to appreciate the humor in this line.) You are looking for someone who can bring out the best in everyone else. That is key. You are not looking for a shooting guard or a small forward. You are looking for a point guard with special skills. You are looking for people playing the right positions.

You have to know your people (team). You have to know their skills. You have to know what motivates them. I think a good leader knows her people well. A good leader is one who enables others to lead.

Here is a little more advice from my experience in athletic administration on delegating: A mental road block to delegation can be, "If you want it done right, do it your-self." Remember though, you're not the only person who can do things right. Some people are uncomfortable asking for help. Maybe you feel that you're supposed to be able to handle everything. If you view asking for help as a weakness, notice that it's the other way around—trying to do everything is a weakness.

The best example I can think of here is the mile re-lay—the 4x400 meter relay. You need outstanding runners in all four legs to win this race. Everyone needs to hit her mark. And the exchange is so important—handing off the baton from one person to another.

The person to whom you delegate will make mistakes. Don't delegate a task assuming the other person will ex-ecute it perfectly until she has a proven track record. When you train someone to do something, you're making an investment.

Recognize and praise the efforts of others on your be-half. When someone does something for you, thank them.

People are more likely to offer to help again if they feel appreciated.

One of the Lady Vols' strongest assets was selling or marketing our program. This was an area in which I loved working with our creative young students and interns. Their ideas were better than those I could have thought of. We were letting the right people develop the ideas.

Delegating not only gets the job done better, but it also breeds competencies. If you ever watched Pat Summitt during a timeout huddle, the first thing she did was listen to her assistant coaches. Each assistant coach had a specific responsibility—offense, defense, game plan, etc. After Pat got the assistant coaches' input at the start of the timeout break, she was able to come up with the best solution for the team. This also made the assistant coaches more responsible and accountable.

Once we had a research team ask to measure Pat's heart rate during a ball game. The time that her heart rate was highest was during this decision point with the assistant coaches. Then when she talked to the team, she had to be calm and her heart rate went down. She went from a higher heart rate gathering information and making a decision to a calmness in teaching the team.

So many times, we think as the leader we are the only ones responsible for motivating our team. Just picture the Lady Vol softball team after a game: win or lose, instead of coaches Ralph and Karen Weekly giving a post-game wrap-up to the team, the team gathers in center field in a circle holding hands and doing what they call "throwing bouquets." Team members complement each other on great plays and things that were significant. The coaches have delegated to the team the responsibility of analyzing the key plays of the game.

It is great to be a part of one of these events. For example, "The hit she made in the third inning got our scoring started." Could you imagine doing this in your office at the end of a project? The throwing of bouquets is a way of pinpointing success—and when the team does it, you are delegating the motivating.

Now, think about a task you might be able to hand off when you are in a crunch.

The blessing of gratitude is happiness.
—Anonymous

It is not happy people who are thankful.
It is thankful people who are happy.
—Anonymous

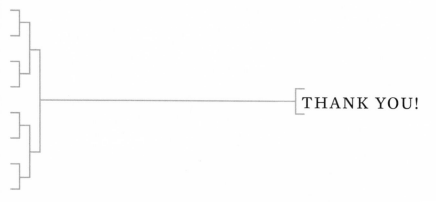

THANK YOU!

I don't think people say thank you enough. It's just a little thing, but it means so much. It is more than etiquette; it is not about some professional standard. For me, it is about one-on-one, person-to-person recognition and acknowledgment.

Does this sound old-fashioned? I don't think so. I think it is in the same category as passing a co-worker in the hallway and saying hello. I would love to see people over-use the phrase "thank you."

My daughter Stacey said, "When my Dad (Tom) was pretty sick in the hospital, he was having a tough time just doing basic tasks. But no matter what, if a nurse, technician, or doctor came in to see him or to perform some check of his vital signs or a procedure to take a blood sample, Dad ALWAYS thanked them. It was amazing to me. It was also a great example of no matter where we are or how we feel . . . we can say, 'Thanks.'"

I am a huge fan of Tennessee football legend Peyton Manning. One of the things I enjoy watching is when, after a great play, he is the first one to tell the receiver or running back "job well done." He gives credit to the team and says thank you.

On another level, it is about saying "I appreciate you," "I appreciate what you did," or "I am simply appreciative in general." Thank-you notes should not be a thing of the past. Emails are nice, but they are not the same as a handwritten letter. But also, don't forget the value of a pat on the back, high five, knuckle bump, or just a smile. Or the hand-written note . . .

Try it for a day or two. See how good it feels. See what kind of responses you get.

I do recognize that "no" is a complete sentence. When you have to say no, doesn't it sound better to say, "No, thank you"?

So many times in the heat of the battle thank you's can be said, but we don't appreciate them because we are just trying to get through the day or the week or the month. Don't we all appreciate when someone comes up to us and says, "Last year, or five years ago, you made a difference in my life"? Doesn't that mean a lot? So, my challenge to you is to write these moments down in thank-you notes to people.

Recently a great article was written about me in the *Athletic Business Journal,* and I got voicemail messages from two people who I respect so much and who are also very, very busy people: Jim Haslam, President of Pilot Oil Company, and Dr. Bob Kaplan, a dermatologist. Both took the time to say "Job well done, Joan!" That meant as much to me as a bouquet of roses.

Kind words mean a lot.

To whom much is given,
much is expected.
—Luke 12:48

GIVING BACK

My responsibility was always to set an example and give back, and you can do that many ways. Going into each new school year speaking to our student-athletes, I felt like these were the four most important things for them to remember:

1. Remember who they are and who they represent— on the floor/court/field as well as Saturday night out on the town.

2. *To whom much is given, much is expected* (Luke 12:48). They as student-athletes were so blessed that I felt it was important for them to give back and set an example for their friends and colleagues. I thought that

maybe I overused 12:48 when one of our former athletes shared the following: "Ms. Cronan, I know you don't like tattoos, but I just got a little one on my wrist. And, it is your favorite Bible verse, Luke 12:48!"

3. You are responsible for yourself and accountable to your team. We are building teams. We don't just watch out for ourselves. If you see one of your teammates about to make a wrong move, it is your responsibility to reach out to them.

4. The only place where success comes before work is in the dictionary. All of our coaches usually instilled this lesson as well.

What do you want your legacy to be?

Recently, Tyler Summitt, son of Pat Summitt and head coach at Louisiana Tech University, tweeted me a quote on the internet. I really liked it. Let me share it with you. The quote was:

> Our character determines our choices.
> Our choices determine our reputation.
> And our reputation determines our legacy.[10]

I think it is so important to try to lead by example. As I tell our athletes and our coaches, I want to be on the front page for winning national championships and doing

---

OPPOSITE: In the Spring of 2015, the city of Knoxville designated Joan Cronan Way, which intersects Neyland Drive on the University of Tennessee campus, to honor Joan's many years of service to the university. Photo by Patrick Murphy-Racey.

great things—not for making mistakes. But I see myself as a servant leader; that is, supporting others to help them meet their goals.

I was standing in line the other day at the post office. The postmaster knows me and he said, "Hey, Joan, the guy behind you makes tombstones, so why don't you tell him what you want on your tombstone?" And I thought, "I really don't want to think about that right now." But I hope they can say I made a difference—that I made a difference in the way I lived my life. It's been my goal. It's been my passion.

My pride is not in what Joan Cronan has done. It is in what the people around me have accomplished and the example we have been at the University of Tennessee in women's athletics. There is a real pride in what our people have accomplished, and I don't think that is a selfish pride. That is the legacy I would hope for—that we did it right, the right way. I'm even pleased they named a street after me and called it the Joan Cronan Way.

Since my official retirement this year, I find myself busier than ever. I asked myself why. The conclusion I come to is that I am trying to turn success into significance. I think I need to realize that I can't do it all in one year.

What is your legacy? I hope that mine is making a difference in young peoples' lives.

It takes a village to raise a Lady Vol . . .
or a good employee . . . or a solid citizen.
—Joan Cronan

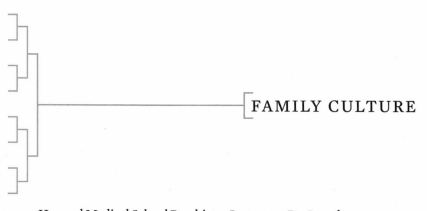

FAMILY CULTURE

Harvard Medical School Psychiatry Instructor Dr. Joseph
Shrand says the family home is the first community. "It's
the social domain that teaches children how to interact
with others. It's hopefully a place where kids begin learning basic rules, values, morals and ethics. In homes where
children feel respected, they go on to do well in the bigger
community."[11]

In the University of Tennessee Women's Athletic Department, we worked to help our kids succeed in a bigger community. We also recognized that socialization oc-
curred in our college community, and we had a series of
special programs designed to create a village of support

that would help these young women succeed in our school and in life.

The Volunteer village included workshops on interviewing techniques, family night, community involvement, basic etiquette lessons, giving-back programs, and academic counseling, to name just a few. We wanted these women to continue to do well in the next bigger communities or villages—in business and in life.

One of the most effective programs we established I actually copied and expanded from a program at the University of Texas. A nice form of flattery is to have someone copy what you are doing. Thank you, Texas. The program we developed was called "guest coaching," and it involved us inviting twelve guests to the University of Tennessee for each Lady Vols home game. I had dinner with the guests prior to the game and talked with them about our program. They went to the locker room during pre-game and at half-time, sat right behind the team during the game, and attended the press conference after the game. This program was designed to do several things: it got people to understand the inner-workings of an athletic program, it rewarded some of our big donors, and it was also a way of introducing new people to our program. Interacting with the coaches and players was instrumental in helping people better understand that "sport is life with the volume turned up."

It is amazing how powerful it is when somebody really gets to know you well in your "home" setting. I suggest you could do this in your business as well.

I believe we all need support and care beyond our immediate families to help us succeed. Rarely can we have all of our needs met in one small circle. This leads to networking and life support—important points for me. But this concept of "it takes a village" can allow us to broaden what author and businessman Stephen Covey calls "spheres of control."[12] For Covey, spheres close to us are manageable. Spheres out of our reach, beyond our control, are the ones to release. Concentrate on the tasks within your sphere or spheres.

It was always important for us to listen to our athletes as well as teach them. Just as a village can offer support to our athletes, so can the simple act of listening. When you listen, it leaves others feeling respected. Respect leads to value, value leads to trust, and trust leads to people reaching their potential. Self-respect leads to self-confidence and strong self-esteem.

What about other forms of community? Fran Walfish, author of *The Self-Aware Parent,* says it does take a village to raise a child and emphasizes the role of the extended family—"the grandparents, aunts and uncles, and cousins who all fill in."[13] I would add that the coach plays an extremely important role in that extended family as well.

We wanted our Lady Vol athletes to have an extended family within their reach. We offered specialized resources including tutors, trainers, team members, and staff members, in addition to coaches and assistant coaches. Our best student-athletes took full advantage of these offerings.

So many times I referred to us as "the Lady Vol family." I took pride in that because it meant our student-athletes were part of an extended family.

Recently I had the opportunity to meet Kevin Plank, founder and CEO of Under Armour. Kevin paraphrased Peter Drucker, well-known educator and management consultant, saying, "Culture eats strategy every morning before breakfast." To me he is saying that the culture around your team or business is more important than game plans.

Kevin also said that you have to "keep the main thing, the main thing." He told me the biggest sign he has in his office that says, "We make T-shirts!"

I can remember talking to a coach about how to deal with a particular athlete. And I said, "Pretend that athlete is my daughter, and you will know what to do."

The most important thing is the next play.
—Coach Mike Krzyzewski,
   Duke University

Don't stop thinking about tomorrow.
Don't stop. It'll soon be here.
—Fleetwood Mac

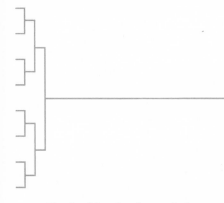

NOT LOOKING BACK

Not looking back reminds me of the line I have used about the best golfers having short memories. This does not mean good golfers forget strokes on their scorecards. It means they can forget a bad shot on the last hole and regroup to hit a better shot on the next hole or the next swing.

The above quote by Coach K indicates: if you make a mistake, acknowledge it, then move on. I'm not promoting a mantra of Eastern religions, where you live totally in the moment, even though not looking back has a Zen-like message to it. But there is a lot of value to being "in the moment" in both sports and life.

I don't think the Duke coach meant all of the previous plays were totally irrelevant, but in the scheme of things, we can't and shouldn't dwell on past mistakes. Shake off an error. Throw off a lost account. Set aside cross words said in a tired moment. Instead, forge ahead. Keep looking upward and onward.

Even if the past behavior or events or plays were big hits, winners, or successes, it still pays to look to the next one. Good news or bad news, we need to keep putting one foot in front of the other.

There was a movie I enjoyed called *City Slickers* starring Billy Crystal. Crystal plays a city slicker taking a week-long vacation trip in the southwest. He meets up with a "cow-poke" who gives him some advice.

The older cowboy tells Crystal, "It's about just one thing." To which Crystal replies, "Oh, yeah, what is that one thing?" Then the older man says to him, "No, dummy! Concentrate on one thing. Become good at just one thing." Gary Keller's book, *The One Thing,* reinforces this point very well. Focus and discipline are necessary. Many of us lack focus. Many of us need more discipline to concentrate on the next play or the one thing.

The book *Outliers* by Malcolm Gladwell emphasizes the importance of repetition to success. Do things 10,000 times before you get a pattern—it's a great learning technique. Being focused takes practice, and it takes work. Yet I encourage you to be more in the moment. Think about now. Even the future can cloud our thoughts or distract us from "the next play."

Fleetwood Mac's famous encourages us: "Don't stop thinking about tomorrow." I really believe it is important to learn from the past and live in the present to build a better tomorrow. Even as a reasonably successful sports administrator, I have gotten blocked at times in my thinking. However, freeing my thoughts—whether on the twelfth fairway or in our executive conference room—really lightened my burden. It made me a better coach, parent, boss, business person . . . and I bet it would help you, too.

> My working life has always been wrapped up in doing my job to the best of my abilities and doing the best for my family. It is not a contest between the two.
> —Johann Lamont

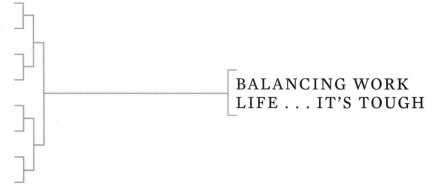

BALANCING WORK LIFE . . . IT'S TOUGH

Okay, we can try. We can work at it.

I got a call a few years back from a friend who said, "Hey, Joan, I've got two Master's tickets for tomorrow's final round. Would you like to have them?" "Wow," I thought. Then I also thought, "It's Easter Sunday."

But we got up really early and celebrated Easter . . . and still made the golf championship.

There's nothing wrong with spur-of-the-moment decisions.

And I've always said I want to have my cake and eat it, too.

In her book *Lean In,* Sheryl Sandberg takes on this topic—balancing one's family and work.[14] She says that choosing the right partner in relationships is the most important decision you make success, because we all need support and balance in both the home and the office.

My husband, Tom, was just that—the very best partner for me. He was always so supportive. Tom and I would be driving along, and I might be stressed out about some small thing that was going on with the Lady Vol program. Tom would make a comment that would bring me back to reality. He would put things into perspective for me.

Tom might say, "Look at all those people over there who are unaware of your problem."

Give these ideas a try to help balance your life the best you can . . .

Keep work and home separate by focusing on your immediate responsibilities where you are. When you are at work, focus on work. Do your best on the task at hand, and try not to be distracted by things going on at home. When you are at home, don't dwell on the fact that you are not at work. There's plenty of time during the work week to accomplish what you need to accomplish.

I do have the ability to focus on one thing at a time—to be in the present moment. This has helped me a great deal. It is so important, being able to focus on what you are doing now and not thinking about another thing you need to do after this meeting.

One more thought here. Think about yourself playing golf for four hours. A lot of that time is spent driving, walking, and getting ready to make a shot. The actual drive or putt just takes maybe thirty seconds. But sometimes our brain keeps us from concentrating on that shot. It is one of the main reasons we are out there—to hit that white ball successfully. Yet even though the shots are our point of focus, we are often distracted during that crucial time. That lack of focus may keep us from doing what we are there to do.

As a leader, it is so important that you keep your life balanced. I don't want anyone to out-work me, but we all need to strive for balance. I think vacations are important.

Northwestern's Jim Phillips is a successful athletics director, and he was a former assistant athletics director for UT. One Sunday morning when I came by the office to meet with a recruit, Jim, at that time a young father of four, was in his office. Rather than being impressed, I talked to Jim about priorities other than UT. It turned out to be a good lesson for him. And I know he applies it now.

So this sets a tone or an environment for your people. I encouraged families to be a part of the job when possible. I always loved the opportunity for Pat Summitt's son, Tyler, to be part of the team when we were competing. He brought some reality to what we were doing.

I think one of the most important responsibilities we have in our lives is our children. They should be a priority. I was always proud and excited to include my family in some of the experiences I had as an athletics director. They had an opportunity to see the world and outstanding athletic events.

I am fortunate to be blessed with two daughters who are now my best friends. Sure, the teen years are challenging. And I think I saw some of my stubbornness in my daughters. But isn't it great to have such strong women as a result?

And one of the blessings of children is grandchildren. As I journey into this phase of my life, I've found that grandchildren are an additional blessing.

Susan Packard talks about me in the introduction of her new book, *New Rules of the Game: Ten Lessons for Women in the Workplace.* It's a nice reference. Flattering—especially coming from someone as sharp as she is. She talks about the importance of competition and the art of gamesmanship. Gamesmanship is about the desire to compete and win.

I think life has different seasons, and sometimes that means different priorities.

To avoid overextending yourself, create one main calendar for home and work commitments. Include everything—recitals, family dinners, work meetings. Having one place where you keep track of all of your important details can help you to manage them better.

Life can be challenging, especially when balancing responsibilities. Sometimes everything at work and at home may seem to happen at once. Things can build up until you can't handle much more. In times like those, let some things go.

I was at a meeting recently, and the speaker asked the audience, "If you could re-live your career what would you do differently?" Well, one person spoke up and said something that I thought was quite profound. She said that she would have taken better care of herself, so that she could take better care of others.

Homer Rice, former athletic director at Georgia Tech, talks about the importance of fitness in his most recent book *Leadership Fitness*. Homer was an outstanding leader among leaders in the athletic world.

Though it might be tempting to schedule every hour, it is important for you to keep some down time in your life. Leave a little time each day to rest. Remember that allowing yourself to recharge will not only help you feel better—it will also help you get your best results.

If you want plenty of experience
in dealing with difficult people,
then have kids.
—Bo Bennett

 DIFFICULT PEOPLE

We spend an incredible amount of time and energy dealing with difficult people. To me it is very important to
keep our core values intact when facing these challenges.
Remember to be yourself in these difficult situations,
because as Abraham Lincoln said, "You can fool all the
people some of the time, and some of the people all the
time, but you cannot fool all the people all the time."

Here are lessons you learn from your children that
help you when faced with challenging personalities.[15]
They are simple but true guidelines for all of us:

1. Stay calm. Take a deep breath.

2. You can't fly like an eagle if you hang out with turkeys. Don't waste your time trying to change a person who has a negative influence.

3. Be proactive. Face problems up front and as quickly as possible.

4. Pick your battles.

5. Separate the person from the issue: "I want to talk about what's on your mind, but I can't do it when you are yelling."

6. Shift the focus from what is wrong to how to solve the problem.

7. Use appropriate humor. Sometimes humor can shine light on the truth and disarm difficult behavior.

8. Change from following to leading. In a healthy conversation, two people take turns leading and following.

9. Confront bullies. When victims stand up for their rights, bullies will often back down.

10. Set consequences. This is a skill that can cause a difficult person to stand down.

And a few more simple suggestions . . . [16]

1. Don't get dragged down. Don't let someone else's negative views drag you down.

2. Listen. You may feel like tuning this person out, but listen so they will see someone who cares.

3. Use a time limit for venting. Allow the upset person a short time to vent. Then move on to what is next.

4. Don't agree. Agreeing will only encourage the negative person.

5. Don't stay silent. This could be interpreted as agreement.

Whatever type of person you find challenging to work with, it is important to be aware of their styles, as well as to make efforts to adapt to this person's way of communicating.

One of my all-time favorite coaches is soccer coach Angie Kelly, who won four national championships as a player at North Carolina and who was professional soccer player Mia Hamm's roommate. Angie understood the importance of being hard-nosed and competitive. I can remember her theme one year was "Leave your drama to your mama." The team did—and they won the SEC Championship.

So, it is important to gain an awareness of your own communication style. Then, you must develop an awareness of the person with whom you are trying to work effectively. Where do you miscommunicate with your messages? How could you better connect? When we speak to someone's style, we can better connect with them. This may be the single biggest barrier to making progress.

I'll close this section with one more example from my experience. There is a book entitled *The No Asshole Rule: Building a Civilized Workplace and Surviving One*

That Isn't. It was written by Stanford University Professor Robert I. Sutton, and it sold 100,000 copies and won the Quill Award for best business book in 2007. I gave a copy of this book to employees I was having a difficult time with and I said, "Read this and let's talk about it tomorrow."[17]

They seemed to get the point, and it was easier than having a long, painful series of meetings.

You can get by on charm
for about 15 minutes. After that,
you better know something.
—H. Jackson Brown, Jr.

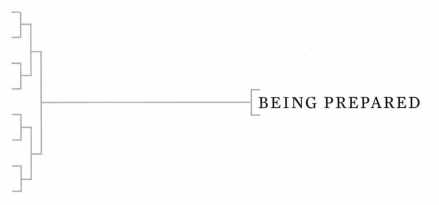

BEING PREPARED

As you know, my career was spent in college athletics, which has been primarily a man's world. Thus, I always felt like I had to be more prepared than anyone else. I also always felt that as a woman I needed to work harder than the men around me. I'm not sure exactly why. Maybe I had to prove that I should be there. Maybe it is my truly competitive nature. I don't know.

I do know I had to adapt and be prepared to fit into a different environment at times. It wasn't always easy.

Don't get me wrong; I like males. It's just a different kind of meeting when you are the only female in the session. It's not a bad thing, either; just a thing. I always felt that I had an obligation to do well because I wanted in the future to see more women in the boardroom.

Let's see if I can prepare you for a boardroom meeting where you are the only female among all males.

I can remember a time when, in negotiating a new television contract for the SEC, each presenter started with the line, "you guys and Joan." After a few presenters said this, I called timeout. And I indicated to all that it did not bother me at all to be referred to as "you guys." And I mentioned to them that when I was coaching, I never used a woman-to-woman defense. We played man-to-man defense.

I think being prepared and being willing to adapt to different work settings has helped me, too. And I do have to share with you a story about adapting from my career. It is a light story that did not take place in the boardroom, but I must share it with you:

The Lady Vol volleyball team made it to the regional finals a few years back. It turned out to be the same weekend as an SEC football championship game in Atlanta. And the UT band wanted to go to Atlanta. So I called Minnesota and rented their ice hockey band. (Minnesota was the school where the volleyball team was going to play.) We sent them orange shirts and the music to "Rocky Top," and they played "Rocky Top." They played "Rocky Top" a lot. They played it very well.

OKAY, NOW FAST FORWARD.

Minnesota played Alabama that year in the 2004 Music City Bowl in Nashville. They beat Alabama. It was a big win for their school. At the end, to rub it in, their band played "Rocky Top." And their band played "Rocky Top" . . . and their band played "Rocky Top" . . . I guess they learned that song very well.

But back to being prepared. Being prepared also refers to "think before you speak." It is often said: A fool may talk, but a wise man speaks. It's important to say something worthwhile when you do speak up, whether you are a woman speaking to all males or one-on-one with your best friend.

There's that, and there's also one more thing to prepare for: the future.

Stay up-to-date with technology. Use it to your advantage in your job. Do not be afraid of iPads and attachments and PDFs. Technology is so important these days; we have to keep up. It isn't easy—just new versions of software alone are a challenge. I try hard to keep pace because I know it is important. I think it keeps me on the same page or sometimes even a few pages ahead of the people I work with. Maybe this advice can encourage you to work at it, too.

According to Jane Hight McMurry, in her book *Navigating the Lipstick Jungle*, "Technology is like a piano. You won't get any music from it unless you play it."[18]

People don't care how much
you know until they know how
much you care.
—John Maxwell

CONNECTING

I will never forget when I interviewed for the UT athletics director position. After a very intense lunch interview with people on the search committee, Ann Furrow, a UT Board of Trustees member, was assigned to take me to the next meeting. She asked me two questions, which in today's legalistic world would probably not be appropriate. But thirty years later, I still remember what she said.

1. She said, "From the way you answered your questions I assume you are a strong Christian." And,

2. "If you accept this position, what will this mean to Tom (my husband)?"

This told me that she cared about me as a person and that she cared about my family. And I wanted to be associated with people like that.

In my job, I have had to deal with many different types of people. I felt like the school principal at times. You know, high school principals must work with parents, students, teachers, the public, and administrators, just to name a few.

As women's athletics director, I came in contact with recruits, athletes, coaches, fans, donors, suppliers/vendors, businesses, staff members, other schools, and many others on a daily basis. It was crucial for me to connect with them quickly and effectively. Often they were coming at me from different directions with different agendas, too. Communicating successfully with all of these different audiences was a key factor to my success.

I liked that part of my job. I hope I learned to do it well. At least that was the feedback I received from others.

The following three statements may sound a little self-serving, but they do show three different perspectives and the importance of communication.

1. One of my bosses, UT President Emeritus Joe Johnson, said, "Joan was a wonderful face for women's athletics. Even at events like the SEC Tournaments, Joan was always the person talking to the crowd. You would have thought she was running for governor."

2. Former UT Board of Trustees member and Lady Vol development director Susan

Speaking at long-time coach Nancy Wilson's retirement at the College of Charleston. Courtesy College of Charleston photographer.

Williams said, "Let me tell you, Joan Cronan made a difference at UT and at a national level for women's sports. She was a unique leader in a unique position."

3. "Joan is very much a people person. All Lady Vol sports were a beneficiary of that," said Donna Thomas, athletic administration co-worker. "Joan was very successful. She has a charisma about her that draws people to her."

A key factor that separates high achievers from others is strong communication skills. If you work with people, communicating with them is important. From a car mechanic to a nuclear physicist, the ability to communicate with others gains respect, admiration, and often more business. No matter how competent you are in your work, without the ability to express yourself, other skills might go unnoticed.

Larry King, a poor kid from Brooklyn, was widely known as "the mouthpiece." He talked his way into his first radio job and continued to talk his way to stardom—whether you agreed with what he said or not.

In his book, *Talk with Anyone, Anytime, Anywhere,* King tells personal stories about communicators he has interviewed.[19] You'll hear secrets that made Mario Cuomo and John Kennedy powerful political speakers, Ted Turner and Ross Perot dynamic businessmen, and George Burns and Bob Hope . . . well, funny. If you think you were born without the gift of gab, you can improve your speaking abilities. Here are a few words of advice in this area:

1. Be confident: you have something to say
2. Listen to customers and employers
3. Be prepared with good questions
4. Speak up in meetings
5. Overcome shyness
6. Use appropriate humor in speaking

Many people feel uncomfortable in a social setting, believing they do not know what to say. People fear small talk. But it is possible to have an excellent conversation by getting the other person to do most of the talking. The pressure is off you when you focus on the other person. People who lack confidence are inward focused. If you worry that you are uninteresting, you fail to connect because you are too concerned about how you come across.

Gold medals aren't really made of gold.
They're made of sweat, determination,
and a hard-to-find alloy called guts.
—Dan Gable

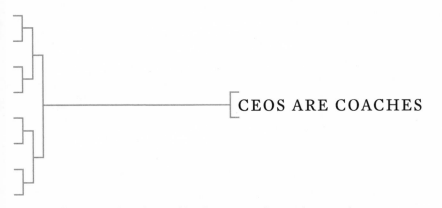

CEOS ARE COACHES

I often considered myself to be a sort of consultant and cheerleader. According to Tom Peters, author of *A Passion for Excellence*, a good leader is both a cheerleader and a nurturer of champions.[20] As the athletics director for the Lady Vols, part of my job was to coach the coaches. Fortunately, I was able to hire great people, and so we spent most of our time tweaking things. It wasn't the basic skills they needed help with, though: it was the icing on the cake.

Reflecting on his Gallup research, best-selling author Marcus Buckingham says, "The corporate world is bad at capitalizing on the strengths of people."[21] Managers clearly need to engage the hearts and the minds of both the individual and the team.

Coaching fulfills this need. Buckingham says that leading as a coach means letting go of control from a distance. Individuals and teams must understand the organization's direction and be empowered to work toward it using their best capabilities.

You can increase your people's performance with effective coaching. Stats show that organizations who train leaders to be effective coaches have higher levels of employee productivity and increased employee engagement.

As the leader becomes a coach, the leadership role shifts to one of shaping understanding, development, and learning. Consider a study conducted in a large pharmaceutical company where the competencies for leadership were compared with the competencies of a coach. The result? Seventy-five percent of the competencies were the same. To be an effective leader, it helps to be an effective coach.

Here are some ideas from professionals regarding the skills needed to coach:

Martha Duesterhoft, who works on the leadership team at a business-strategy company called PeopleResults, suggests more asking instead of telling, more developing and learning, more focus on desired goals, and more being in the moment.[22]

Yael Bacharach, co-founder and director of training at the Bacharach Leadership Group, recommends better listening, taking in what you hear, reflecting with accuracy, and providing feedback for development.[23] Bacharach wrote about these coaching skills in *Inc. Magazine* in 2013.

And as Larry King said, "I never learned anything while I was talking."

We have two Lady Vol teams that are coached by husband and wife teams. Mike Patrick and Sandra Hahn-Patrick coach the Lady Vol tennis team, and Ralph and Karen Weekly coach the Lady Vol softball team. Both pairs have done incredible jobs. I am very proud of these coaches. I have observed how they coach each other, and in both cases, they bring out the best in each other. That's what good coaches do.

In conclusion, please consider the questions below. Part 1—People:

1. What could you do to strengthen your network?
2. How could you enable others to trust you more?
3. Think of a task you might be willing to delegate. What is that task? Who might you involve or call on to complete it?
4. For whom are you thankful?
5. What is your legacy?
6. Are there any ideas from the Lady Vol family that you might use in your workplace?
7. Is there something you should let go of or forgive yourself for?
8. What could you do to help balance work and life?
9. Think about the person(s) with whom you have difficulty. Where do you clash?
10. Where could you improve your own communication skills?

2

PRIDE

Pride (definition): A feeling of deep pleasure or satisfaction derived from one's own achievements, the achievements of those with whom one is closely associated, or from qualities or possessions that are widely admired. E.g., the team was bursting with pride after recording a sensational victory.

As I mentioned in the introduction to the People section, ESPN requested an interview with me a few years ago. They wanted me to tell them the keys to the Tennessee Lady Vols' success. I was ready to give them a thirty-minute speech, but they wanted a sound bite. So I said I thought the key to our success was developing a pride and a passion for the Lady Vols. And, you know—it is the same way you do it in your business.

I love to watch women's basketball and see players pull the front of their jersey out to the camera. It shows their team's name more clearly. That is pride. To me, she is a player showing that her team name is more important than her individual name on the back of her shirt.

It has been fun to watch the pride factor built into the phrase "Lady Vols." I am extremely conscious of our pride factor, and it is something that I want to take care of. I want to embrace that pride and be sure that we always live up to it—and the standards are high. Our pride at the University of Tennessee is very visible; it is Big Orange Country and we love our "Rocky Top." Pride emerges in different ways for different reasons.

Sometimes pride is motivated by external drivers, as was the case for Mark Zuckerberg, inventor of Facebook.

He did not start Facebook only to connect millions of people all over the world, nor did he found his multibillion-dollar company solely for the money, judging by his trademark jeans and hoodie sweatshirt. He did it, author Ben Mezrich implies in *The Accidental Billionaires,* because he wanted to show up a girl who dumped him and get back at the guys in Harvard's most elitist social club.[24] The desire to prove he was smarter than they were gave Zuckerberg the motivation he needed to start on a path toward becoming one of the world's preeminent innovators.

As a foreshadowing, in this section are the three C's—confidence, competition, and communication. I have included some of my favorite thoughts for motivating myself and others to a sense of pride that becomes contagious for all of us. There are also a couple of pieces in this section that are very personal to me, including several nuggets from my two daughters. I hope you enjoy reading it as much as I enjoyed putting it together.

If you keep your chin up,
you are not bowing your head
in defeat or sadness.
—October 1900,
  the *Evening Journal* (PA)

CHIN UP

Never let your opponent see you sweat.

"Keep your chin up. Don't take your troubles to bed with you. Hang them on a chair with your trousers." That's what the *Evening Journal* article said in the fall of 1900.[25]

In one of today's most popular books, author and technology executive Sheryl Sandberg writes about *Lean In*—a physical gesture to encourage positive outcomes. *Lean In* is one of the best books I have read about women being successful.

This past Christmas both of my daughters, Kristi and Stacey, gave me a specially made copper and silver bracelet with the words "Chin Up" inscribed on it. The girls

My Chin Up bracelet was a gift from my daughters Stacey and Kristi. They said I was encouraging to them even before the book *Lean In* by Sheryl Sandberg became a hit. My advice was always keeping your chin up. Photo by Patrick Murphy-Racey.

said to me, "Sandberg may be talking about *Lean In*, but you always told us to keep our chin up."

To me, what that bracelet stood for was even better than the bracelet itself.

Since they were little girls, I had told my daughters to keep their chins up. I think it is so important. Your body language conveys more than you think.

For my wonderful daughters—both graduates of Knoxville West High School and the University of Tennessee (with Human Ecology majors)—to bring this message back to me . . . wow, it was so nice. Kristi Benner, my older daughter by 19 months, lives in Charlotte, North Carolina. She works as a recruiter for an executive search firm called Recruit UP, LLC (based in Greenville, South Carolina). My younger daughter, Stacey Bristow, lives in Knoxville. Stacey has worked in the hospitality business and taught family and consumer science. She presently serves on the board for the Christian Academy of Knoxville (CAK). And she is a tester and educator with Samaritan Ministries.

A few more thoughts on Chin Up before we turn our cheeks and move ahead:

When competing in tennis, I never wanted to let my opponent see me getting tired or frustrated. It was important to keep my chin up! I always felt that I needed to have a look of confidence. More information later about the *Inner Game of Tennis* . . .[26]

As a leader at the University of Tennessee, I always thought it was good to call our coaches when good things happened—like a big win. But I also felt that when things didn't go quite as well, I should also call them and give them some words of encouragement. Lady Vol softball co-head coach Karen Weekly brought this up recently. She said that she was always appreciative of a "chin-up" phone call from me after a tough loss as well as a key win.

To me, keeping your chin up is all about attitude. And it goes back to one of my pet peeves in communication: negative body language. I don't like being around people who keep their head down, who never look you in the eye, and who never smile. This gives off such negative vibrations.

We all have people we work with who, when we see them coming, make us want to go the other way. Sheryl Sandberg says, "Lean in with confidence," and I say, "Keep your chin up and look forward"—be it rain or sunshine ahead.

Arriving at one goal is the starting
point to another.
—John Dewey

A goal is a dream with a deadline.
—Napoleon Hill

GOALS

What is your plan for setting goals? Do you have one?
There is a lot of value in going through this process, you
know . . .

I had not set out to be Athletics Director of the Year in
a certain number of years when I took my first AD job at
the College of Charleston. I did, however, set short-term
goals to address staff needs, create a reasonable budget,
raise funds, and develop winning programs. I will tell you
that I wanted to be an athletics director at an early age. I
think I was twelve years old when I first realized this.

I went to try out for Little League. I was ready. I had
my ball and glove. I had been practicing. But they told me

in no uncertain terms, "Girls don't play!" What a shock. They said I could take care of the equipment. They said I could keep score. Baloney! I wanted to play. I was going to have to fix that. It took a few years.

I identified important work goals that tied to key parts of our business. Meanwhile, I identified important personal goals that tied to key parts of my life.

I also . . .

1. Stated why my goals were worthwhile
2. Asked for support to reach my goals
3. Accepted the support of others
4. Revised my goals as I met them
5. Kept track of my progress toward reaching my goals

About keeping score, Pat Summitt said, "We keep score in life because it matters. It counts. Too many people opt out, because they're afraid to commit. They're afraid of failure."

All of these steps helped us reach business goals in our programs and helped me reach personal goals as well.

So, to recap, let me ask these questions:

Is it important?
Do you have someone to go to for help?
How often will you revise your goals?
Do you write down the steps you will take?
What about rewarding yourself for making it to the goal?[27]
This is a good checklist for you, too.

That's a lot of questions. Just take them one at a time. What are some of your goals? As you think about them, consider the questions above.

Also, do you spend your time doing things that will help you reach your goal? You know a goal is a dream with a deadline. Watching more television is not going to help you reach your goal of running a twenty-minute 5K road race. It's going to take some actual, dedicated time running to do that.

I have often been asked what made Pat Summitt such a great basketball coach. I tell people that she was a great teacher; she saw her practices as the classroom. It was the way she spent her time reaching her goals—and helping others reach theirs.

It is not only important that you set your goals but also that you make it a priority to stick to your plan to reach them. Our first goal in our athletic department was to be sure our athletes knew they were a student first and an athlete second. A great example of making this a priority was when Pat Summitt was recruiting a young lady from the coal mining part of Kentucky. She came from a very poor academic and economic area.

In our recruiting world, we can make a home visit and invite the athlete to come to campus. After making the Kentucky home visit, Pat called me on her return trip. She indicated her concern about this athlete succeeding at UT because of her background. The AD in me asked, "How good is she?" Coach Summitt replied, "Very good." I then suggested that we bring her in for a campus visit to see how she would respond to our athletes and coaches.

I will never forget that Saturday morning when 107,000 people dressed in orange were on our campus (obviously a football Saturday). I arrived at my office, and waiting there was a tall, attractive, blonde young lady dressed in one of the most expensive-looking suits I had ever seen. My mind talk kept picturing her economic background, so during the visit I said, "That is one of the most attractive suits I have ever seen." She smiled and said, "My mother drew a picture of the suit Pat Summitt had on during her visit with us. And she made this suit for me to visit Tennessee." Needless to say, I wanted her to be a Lady Vol immediately. We had already made a difference in her life.

During her freshman and sophomore years she did very well academically and athletically. She was not the star, but she was really a great blue-collar worker. In February during the most intense SEC competition, her academic advisor came to me and indicated that she was struggling academically. It wasn't that she was not trying; it was like she was on a treadmill and couldn't catch up. So I called a summit conference with the athlete, Pat, and our academic advisor.

We decided we would pull her off the road and out of practice for three weeks to give her time to catch up. But to show her we were not punishing her, we let her start at every home game. After two weeks our academic advisor gave her a thumbs up to begin practicing and travelling again.

That year we went to the SEC tournament and our team lost in the finals, but she made the all-tournament team. I was so glad we had not denied her an opportunity to be the best that she could be.

Fast forward to the Final Four that year. We were getting ready to play in the semi-final game. In the hotel I was busy taking care of athletics director duties—tickets, alumni receptions, donor and president arrivals, etc. I ran back to my room to change clothes for the game, and my phone rang. It was this young lady crying. She wanted me to be the first to know that UT had just called and she had made the dean's list. She went on to help us win a national championship.

The next year, she became the first member of her family to graduate from college. I am so glad that we set our goals and stuck with them—student first, athlete second.

Setting goals is important throughout life even as our perspectives and priorities change with age. Bob Buford talks about the second stage of life or career in his book *Halftime: Moving from Success to Significance*. Buford says that later in your career or life, it may be more important for you to turn your success into significance. He says that your goals may be more about making a difference than about making a name at that point in your life.

I want to turn success into significance. I hope to use some of my successes to reach significance. I've looked at my career as a journey. I've enjoyed it from not being able to participate in Little League to being involved at the highest level. My goal in the journey has been to develop a road map for others to follow, and I think we are going to see more success in the future with young women being able to take over leadership roles—not only in athletics, but in the boardroom—because of what they have learned in sports.

As I look back at my time an administrator, my goal was always to develop a winning team and reach the highest success level possible. As I approach the opportunity now to serve on boards, consult with businesses, and chair programs such as Leadership Knoxville, I think about how this relates.

It's all about putting the right people in the right positions and giving them the tools to be successful. By tools I mean setting goals, motivating the team, praising them, giving them a swift kick in the rear when necessary—and having everybody feel a part of the championship. (If you haven't read *Energy Bus* by Jon Gordon I highly recommend it.)

So at this stage it's not just about winning games; it's about making a difference for people in our community.

> Everyone thinks of changing the world,
> but no one thinks of changing himself.
> —Leo Tolstoy

CHANGE

A graduate student came into my office in Thompson-Boling Arena a few years ago and told me she wanted to become an athletics director. But she had a few questions for me. She asked, "Do you think I will have to move away from my hometown to get a good job? And also, will I have to get up in front of people and speak very often?"

Guess what? That woman is an outstanding accountant with a "big five" accounting firm today.

As an athletics director it has been necessary for me to:

1. Move away from my hometown—Opelousas, Louisiana—with stops in Baton Rouge, Natchitoches, Charleston, and Knoxville along the way, and
2. Speak to different groups daily, including department staff, fans, athletes, coaches, university administrators, corporations, sales staffs, and government agencies.

Sometimes we have to deal with change in our lives in order to meet our goals—to be successful in our careers. And you know, it doesn't matter whether you work in sports administration as I did or in some other area of business. Change is life. Life is change. Sometimes we do not want it and even resist it, while other times we demand it.

Sometimes changes come at you all at once, and sometimes they are spread out over time—years even. Sometimes the changes are in our personal lives, and sometimes they are mixed between personal and professional lives. We might choose the change ourselves or have it thrust upon us; it does not matter. Either way, we need to accept things and move ahead, and we must also remember to enjoy the journey. Sometimes we set our expectations so high in life that we forget to enjoy the steps to reach our goals.

My journey as a college athletic administrator was affected greatly by the passage of Title IX in 1972. This federal law required equal opportunity for both men and women in athletics. The changes it brought about have made an impact on the way people address equal opportunity.

Popular *Knoxville News Sentinel* cartoonist Charlie Daniel depicted me as Joan of Arc in a feature cartoon after I was appointed University of Tennessee Athletics Director. Courtesy Charlie Daniel, *Knoxville News Sentinel.*

The journey required patience, persistence, negotiation, and a tremendous amount of communication and trust. The change brought about by Title IX will have long-lasting effects on competitive opportunities for women.

I have had to deal with changes quickly numerous times in my life. It has helped me to be ready. In basketball, you can't wait too long to change from a man-to-man to a zone defense; if you do, the game will be over.

One of the most visible times of change is when a coach calls a timeout. They motivate, provide constructive criticism, pat somebody on the back, and possibly change offense and defense, all in thirty seconds.

Remember—sport is life with the volume turned up.

> What you do speaks so loudly
> that I cannot hear what you say.
> —Henry David Thoreau

WALKING THE TALK

Do what you say you are going to do. Walk the talk.

A good supervisor will tell you this—so will a good parent.

If I were there with you, I might have even caught you nodding your head "yes." Go ahead. Admit it. You think actions speak louder than words.

This is a really fundamental trait, but oh, so important. Call it what you will—aligning your values with your actions—being clean about things (saying and doing). It's a big deal.

Dale Carnegie used to say that we all ask three basic questions about someone (if not verbally, then mentally) when we meet them:[28]

Can I trust you?

Do you know what you are talking about?

And, do you care about me personally?

"Are you going to do what you said you were going to do?" covers questions such as "Can I count on you?" and "Have you got my back?" I've been told that these are two of the things recruits ask of coaches; I know they are things my coaches asked of me. And I bet they are things your employees, customers, and family members ask of you, too!

The flip side of this idea is "do what I say, not what I do." But that doesn't work—you have to live what you preach. So many times you hear people talk about the student-athlete, but then they forget the "student" part. I am as proud of the Lady Vol graduation rate as of the conference and national championships.

Our policy was that you sat in the first three rows of class, and if you missed a class, you missed a competition. I think that could have been the reason Pat Summitt achieved a one hundred percent graduation rate during forty years of coaching—and I think that is walking the walk and not just talking the talk.

Practice what you preach, walk your talk, match your actions and words, say what you are going to do and do what you say you are going to do, be consistent, and keep your promises: these are all different ways of saying the same thing—have integrity. Simon Sinek wrote a great book in 2014 called *Leaders Eat Last*, which emphasizes the same points about integrity.

My responsibility is leadership,
and the minute I get negative,
that is going to have an influence
on my team.
—Don Shula

LEGACY

Totally independent of each other, my two daughters, Stacey and Kristi, said that they admired similar things about me:

Stacey: "I could talk for hours about things that I admire about her. She is always positive no matter what is going on. In fact, we called her Pollyanna because she is so positive."

Kristi: "I love talking about mom! I admire her positivity. She is one of the most positive individuals. In different situations in life that came up, she would always see the good."

The Cronan clan enjoy time together in the University of Tennessee Athletic Director sky box at a UT football game. Courtesy Joan Cronan.

I am so proud of their comments. They are wonderful women. I want to emphasize the importance of being positive. My daughters helped me say it. They also added a few more things. Who am I to hold them back?

Stacey: "Mom is a hard worker. She always has been. She is a goal setter, a list-maker, and an ethical woman. She lives by the golden rule."

Kristi: "She said 'do unto others' and she lived by it."

Stacey: "Even with all her success, she is grounded and she made family a priority."

Kristi: "She handles things as they come up. She can see the big picture in life. She always said 'remember who you are and who you represent.'"

What greater reward could I have in my life than the admiration of my children? A friend once said, "My father gave me the greatest gift anyone could give another person: He believed in me." My girls believe in me, and I believe in them.

Now that is a feel-good page!

That is my legacy.

Use your head. Make the most
of every chance you get.
—Ephesians 5:15–16

Even if you are on the right track,
you can still get run over.
—Will Rogers

DIRECTION

Successful minister Bob Gass says that following a plan is like using a GPS.[29] If the GPS knows where you are, and you tell it where you want to go, it creates a personalized road map. The difference between a GPS and you is that you have to create all your own step-by-step directions. But that's the fun part—the journey.

Mark Twain said, "The secret of getting ahead is getting started. The secret of getting started is breaking your complex overwhelming tasks into small manageable tasks, and then starting the first one."

Minister Gass prompts us to ask ourselves three questions to help us reach our destination:[30]

1) Where am I?

Jack Welch, the former CEO of General Electric, observed, "Strategic management is trying to understand where you will sit in tomorrow's world, not where you hope to sit; it's assessing where you want to be."[31]

2) Where do I want to go?

What will your dream look like when you've achieved it? Henry Kaiser, founder of Kaiser-Permanente Health Care Company, said, "The evidence is overwhelming that you cannot begin to achieve your best unless you have some aim in life."[32]

3) How will I get there?

Don't expect reaching your destination to be quick or easy. But unless you know where you want to go and identify the steps you must take to get there, years from now you may still be where you are today.

As a coach or leader, you must understand the direction in which your team or business is going. But that is not enough—your teammates need to understand that direction also. It is your responsibility to make sure everyone can read the map.

It was always important for all of us, myself and the coaches, to remember to enjoy the journey. Highly competitive people are so goal-oriented that we forget how important the path is to get to the pot of gold.

Accountability breeds response-ability.
—Stephen Covey

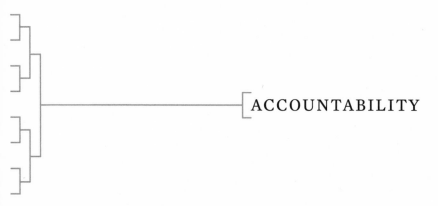

ACCOUNTABILITY

A Lady Vol shortstop gloves a ground ball on the left side but makes the throw to first base a little high—pulling the woman covering first off of the bag. As a result, the opposing team's batter is safe on an error.

One of the things I admire about our shortstop is that she did not yell across the infield at her teammate to reach higher and catch the ball while staying in contact with the base. She didn't throw her glove in the dirt in disgust either. I admire what she did—she lightly pounded her fist on her chest, saying, in effect, "my mistake," "it was my fault," or "I'm sorry to let you down, teammates." She acknowledged her mistake and took ownership of the error.

She was accountable for it, not blaming others or denying she did wrong. She took responsibility and put the error behind her.

It seems that we don't see enough of this in sports or in our lives today. It seems that people would rather say, "I didn't do it. It was someone else's fault." Just think about it. What is the first thing your children say when questioned by you about a situation? "I didn't do anything!" Maybe. What do the suspects always say when they are arrested on the TV show *Law & Order?* "You have the wrong guy. It wasn't me." If we could admit errors, apologize, and move on, outcomes might be better for all.

I have seen work environments where there is little forgiveness. As a result, employees are reluctant to own a mistake. This seems a little rigid. Sure, we want quality and efficient processes and results, but not at the cost of throwing someone else under the bus.

I refer again to Pat Summitt's desire to continuously learn new things. Even after she suffered a loss, she would study new ways to defend an offense that she had not seen before.

As I mentioned earlier, one of the things I told our student-athletes was, "You are responsible for your actions and accountable for your teammates' actions. For example, if you are attending a party and you happen to see a teammate (co-worker) getting out of hand, it's important that you step in and be accountable not only to them but to the rest of the team."

If I am accountable, I can't pass it off. I must own it.

THE 3 C'S

I once heard a speaker say that women need three C's in their lives. I think this applies to men, too, but you'll see from the story why it applies better to women.

The three C's women need in their lives to succeed are as follows:

1. From birth to eighteen years old, we need lots of compliments. If you've ever dealt with teenagers, you know they need lots of positive feedback.

2. From eighteen to thirty years old, we need lots of confidence, because we are making

many big decisions that will last a lifetime (careers, marriage, etc.).

3. After thirty years old, women need CASH. And really, cash, check, or credit card will do.

But really—the three C's that I think you need to succeed in life are confidence, competition, and communication.

Let's look at each of these separately now.

CONFIDENCE

> Life is not easy for any of us. We must have perseverance and above all confidence in ourselves. We must believe that we are gifted for something and that this thing must be attained.
> —Marie Curie

How do you gain confidence?

Learn as much as you can about what you are doing and have a coach or mentor who is going to help you along the way.

Let me tell you a story.

In 1990 the number-two ranked UT Lady Vols were playing the number-one ranked team in the country—the Lady Techsters from Louisiana Tech. Tennessee was behind by one point and there were three seconds left in the game when All-American UT point guard Dena Head was fouled. In a one-plus-one situation, if she hit one foul shot, we would tie. If she hit both foul shots, we would win. Unfortunately she missed the front end of the one-on-one, and we lost the game 59–58.

That was quite a jolt to Dena's confidence. But I watched her respond to the situation—she worked on foul shooting tirelessly during the entire off-season. She practiced and practiced. She was gaining knowledge and gaining confidence because she did not want that situation to happen again.

Then, the next year, the Lady Vols were playing the University of Virginia in the NCAA Championship Game. Virginia was up by seven points near the end of the game when Tennessee got a quick layup and also made a three-pointer. It closed the gap, and we trailed by only two points.

Guess what? Dena got fouled.

The Virginia coach called a timeout to give Dena time to worry about the national championship, the sold-out crowd, the national television audience, the fact that she had to make both shots to tie the game, and what happened the previous year. During the timeout, Tennessee coach Pat Summitt talked about what the team was going to do after Dena made the free throws, giving her confidence by showing that she believed in her.

(Interestingly, Dena left the huddle with lots of confidence. Coach Summitt also knows it's good to have a game plan, so she pulled her center and forward aside and said, "If she misses, this is what you do.")

But with much confidence, Dena made both free throws; Tennessee tied the game and went on to win in overtime, 70–67. The Lady Vols won the national championship in 1991!

It seems to me that this is what confidence is all about. Dena worked very hard to learn from the situation with

Louisiana Tech so that it did not happen again against Virginia. She had a coach and mentor who believed in her.

Let's talk a little more about confidence.

There is an element of risk-taking that goes along with confidence. Not necessarily throwing caution to the wind, but rather an I-can-do-this attitude. Sometimes you can just see it in the way someone walks. Sometimes it is a quiet confidence that is more below the surface.

The person who says they can and the person who says they can't are both right. And as Pat always says, "Attitude is a choice. No one ever got anywhere by being negative."

How does this trait show up? How can you recognize self-confidence?

How do you encourage it and bring it out? Should you?

I think it is important for success in sports and in business.

COMPETITION

> The healthiest competition occurs when average people win by putting out above average effort.
> —Colin Powell

I have always admired retired General Colin Powell, the son of Jamaican immigrants who grew up in the South Bronx. He went on to become a four-star Army general, Chair of the Joint Chiefs of Staff, and the U.S. Secretary of State. Pretty amazing. Powell said, when talking about leadership, "Learn from the pros, observe them, seek them out as mentors and partners."[33] Powell also said to not be afraid to challenge the pros, even in their own backyard.

That is a very competitive spirit.

I believe in competition. I think it goes back to my twelve-year-old experience when I was told by the Little League coach that "girls don't play." I wanted to work in a business that teaches people to compete—teaches women to compete; teaches them to set goals and to reach goals. As a sports administrator, I set general goals to get better. I also set specific goals, such as for our basketball team to reach the Final Four in the NCAA women's basketball tournament.

Let me share something with you. This is one of my favorite readings. I use it often in my speeches:

> I thank my competitors:
> My competitors do more for me than my
>   friends.
> My friends are too polite to point out my
>   weaknesses, but my competitors go to
>   great expense to tell of them.
> My competitors are efficient and diligent.
>   They make me search for ways to
>   improve my products and my services.
> My competitors would take my business
>   away from me if they could. This keeps
>   me alert to hold what I have.
> If I had no competitors, I would be lazy,
>   incompetent, and complacent. I need
>   the discipline they enforce upon me.

I thank my competitors. They have been
   good to me.
GOD BLESS THEM ALL.
(Inspired by Paul Lee Tan)

We get better because somebody is pushing us. Don't be afraid to be competitive.

My friends Anne Sprouse and Sherri Lee and I are very competitive. We bet on whose luggage will come out first in the airport baggage area. I always want to be in the top 10.

It's okay to compete. It's okay to be competitive.

It's not necessary to strong-arm people. Just build relationships and inspire others.

I want to work with people—not against them.

A friend of mine, Robin Green Harris—former Senior Counsel for Ice Miller, and now the Executive Director of the Ivy League Athletics Conference—says:

"Many successful business leaders know, competing in sports provides life lessons that transfer to the executive office. Athletics (organized or informal) teaches leadership skills that are critical to success in the business world. These skills include:

1. Competing to win,
2. Overcoming adversity,
3. Taking risks,
4. Playing with passion, and
5. Working with a team.

Women who participated in sports reported their athletics background helped them advance in their careers in numerous ways. That's consistent with results of a study by the Women's Sports Foundation reporting that 80% of female executives in Fortune 500 companies identified themselves as competitive when they were young.[34]

How about you? Does your competitiveness show? Do you have the drive to win?

Let me tell you about Jane Hill Fleming, a woman I coached in basketball at UT. She went on to the Wharton School of Business and then to a very successful insurance business career. She is really an amazing woman, and I admire her very much.

Jane said, "I learned at an early age that I could compete with anyone. I grew up playing basketball, tennis and softball on the home courts every day after school with the boys in Dandridge, a very small town of barely 2000. (My father refereed and pitched for both sides and I usually beat the boys at almost anything.)

"In high school, our team won the state tournament in basketball before divisions were even established—we were the dark horse and the smallest team in the state (1966). . . . I was MVP. I grew up with the only tennis court in town in my back yard (no school courts or team), so I started winning every tournament I entered as an unseeded player. The growing successes I had in sports built a competitive spirit, a belief that anything is possible, and most importantly, self-confidence. I also understood at an early age the importance of discipline, preparation, teamwork, and training. What more could you need in the business world? It all translated very well," said Fleming.

I believe that to be successful you have to be competitive, and I think sports is a tool that teaches people to be competitive. And you know—today, most women in the top echelons of business competed in athletics.

How competitive are you? What do you think about this trait? Is it important to your success?

COMMUNICATION

> Communication—the human connection—
> is the key to personal and career success.
> —Paul J. Meyer

They say you can't not communicate. What do you think about that?

I want a positive spin here, but first let me state a couple of communication pet peeves that I have . . .

My first pet peeve—say "thank you"! (Please see earlier section. Thank you.)

And my second pet peeve—bad body language. It is important to stand up tall, look the audience in the eye, and keep your chin up.

Okay, I feel better. I have expressed a few of my communication needs.

Now, let's talk a little more about this topic. I want to communicate with my team. It is very important. I even think that time spent talking at the water cooler in the office can be time well spent.

Mike Levesque, one of my partners in DIREC Consulting, complimented me. He said that I needed to read the book *TouchPoints* because it sounded like my management style.

In *TouchPoints*, Douglas Conant and Mette Norgaard emphasize communicating with the team. I agree with the authors that everyone is essential to the team and that everybody needs to know the leader realizes they are important. Some people think that interacting with their team causes too much interruption, but I disagree. It could be the most important thing you do.

I also believe that it is important to spend time with people instead of just rushing through your conversations. The interactions should be meaningful. I have often been told that I don't sit down at basketball games. I don't. I have felt that game time is one of the most important times to interact with our fans and donors.

I remember after one particular overtime game, Pat called me at home and said she saw me visiting with a fan during an intense part of the game. I told her I had taped the game and would watch it when I got home that night, but I wouldn't have had the opportunity to raise funds and visit with the fans after the game. Pat immediately said, "You keep raising money and I'll coach the team." That's a good partnership!

You have to take time to get to know your team—athletic team, work team, family team. You must communicate to the team and to each member on the team.

To know the team better, we always had "family night" for the Lady Vols. At family night, the women brought pictures of their families and loved ones. The basketball team always did it in the locker room, and it really brought the team closer.

Here is another cool lesson about communicating from a book called *The Rhythm of Life* by Matthew Kelly:

> Let others talk.
> Avoid arguments.
> Don't complain.
> Give honest and sincere compliments.
> Be more ready to compliment than to criticize.[35]

A couple of my favorite quotes by Mark Twain are: "If you have nothing to say, say nothing," and "it is better to keep your mouth closed and have people think you are a fool than to open it and remove all doubt."

Have you ever been in a conversation and had to say, "No wait, that's not what I meant"? You probably thought you had made yourself clear with what you just said. What happened? What got between you and the person you were talking to?

I have worked hard on communication skills all throughout my career—really. I have made it a priority to at least try to communicate effectively. Sometimes, though, I think the more I know the less I understand about it. It certainly does take time and care to communicate well.

Even tone of voice can change a message. Read the sentence below three times. Each time you read it, place more emphasis first on "she," then on "stole," and then on "money."

I did not say *she stole* the *money*.

Placing emphasis on one word can change the meaning of the entire message. Emphasizing "she" in the sentence implies someone else stole the money; emphasizing "stole" assumes she did something to the money, but maybe she borrowed or earned it instead of stealing. Emphasizing "money" implies she stole something but it wasn't money. Isn't that amazing?

It certainly shows the importance of feedback—words do things! Perhaps every now and then we should say something like, "Was that clear?" Or maybe, "Would you repeat that back to me to make sure we have a clear understanding?"

I also think the key here is knowing who you are communicating to. Think about this: during a game, a basketball coach calls timeout. That coach has thirty seconds to communicate, and that coach has to understand each player. That coach has to know which one needs a kick, which one needs praise, who responds to a challenge, and so on. Words have to get specific things done.

This all has to happen under pressure during a short timeout. Sport is life with the volume turned up.

And, oh yes, don't forget to respond quickly to people who leave you messages. May I suggest listening to their message and calling them back immediately? Recently I received a very negative voice mail. I immediately pushed the "return call" button and could tell the person was shocked that I called back—but we probably had a better conversation then than we would have at the end of the day. In sports terms, I took the offense away from him.

I once worked with a coach who unfortunately used inappropriate language in coaching his team. To me this is not the way to communicate. I communicated that to him by saying, "You are smarter than that, so improve your vocabulary."

In conclusion, I don't think the three C's to success are cash, check, and credit card, but rather confidence, competition, and communication. Although, of course, a little cash along the way doesn't hurt.

Once again, I want you to apply ideas from this written work to your own personal and professional life. Below are a few questions for you to think about relating to Part 2 —Pride:

1. When do you most need to keep your chin up?
2. What is your plan for setting goals?
3. What are your own barriers to dealing with change that you must overcome to meet your goals?
4. Do you do what you say you are going to do?
5. Do you think about your legacy?
6. Where are you going—seriously?
7. Are you accountable for your own actions?
8. Do you project confidence?
9. Are you competitive?
10. How well do you communicate?

3

PASSION

There are so many aspects to being an athletics director. I get asked, "What does an athletics director do?" It's hard to describe, but I usually say that my job is to make the coach's job the best it can be and to make the experience of the athletes the best it can be. The key thing is making a difference in young people's lives.

If I were the president of Xerox, my product would be a copying machine. But as women's athletics director, my product is the education of the young ladies we get to work with day in and day out. I tell the parents of these young ladies that they are sending us their most prized possession and that it is our job to mold and further develop what they and their hometowns have given us.

I tell these women that I want them to be an all-American; I want them to win national championships; and I want them to graduate. But I also want them to walk out of our program in what I call "the Tennessee way"—as a Lady Vol representing us for the rest of their lives.

What helping others has done for me is fulfill a dream. I talk about this a lot, but it is important to me. I grew up (and you can catch my Cajun accent) in Opelousas, Louisiana—and I have to admit, it took until the third grade for me to learn to spell that. Barbara Mandrell had a song that said, "I was Country, when Country wasn't cool." Well, I was a tomboy before it was cool for women to be in sports. I was twelve years old when I tried out for Little League baseball and they wouldn't let me play. The guy was really nice; he offered to let me be a cheerleader, a manager, an assistant coach—but he wouldn't let me play. I knew then I wanted to be in a business that taught women to compete. This is where some of my passion comes from.

I have to say that the key ingredients for success are passion and pride, and I truly have a passion for making a difference in women's lives. I have been blessed to be in a situation to make that difference.

The most important thing
in life is knowing the most
important things in life.
—David F. Jakielo

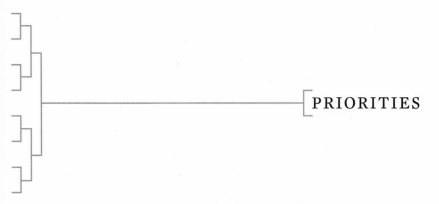 PRIORITIES

Think about your typical day. Think about what you do.

What is your style of work? Which of these work styles, listed in the next sentence, sound most like you? Task hopper, super perfectionist, fence-sitter, very detailed, cliff-hanger, maybe even something else . . .

Does knowing your time management style help you to better understand how you work or how you do your work?

Think about this concept. Could you use other resources (people) to help?

Let's use a round figure for an example. If you make $100,000 per year and you work about 2,000 hours per year (the average is 2,080 hours per year)—that comes out to fifty dollars an hour.

Could a task be handled another way or by someone other than you? It might cost less or be more efficient—it could take less hours. It is worth considering. Maybe you have a new idea to work with already. We already talked more about delegation in a previous section.

But let's go back to priorities. How about your priorities—are they clear? Do you know what you should be spending your time on at work? I suggest that this is a good time to re-read the BELLS section in the prologue. Are you making the BELLS ring?

How about these questions: what tasks do you spend most of your time on? Have you ever tracked this?

Most people spend eighty percent of their time on about twenty percent of their tasks, according to Austrian economist Vilfredo Pareto. But the main point is that there are some tasks that are particularly key to your job. These tasks are probably what you do best.

Marketing people know that about eighty percent of their product is purchased by twenty percent of their audience. The Lady Vols at UT knew this. We knew our audience of customers and supporters very well. It was certainly important to our ongoing success.

The business side of athletics can be divided into three parts, each of which is important. It is not only about wins and losses; it is:

1. Education,
2. Finance, and
3. Entertainment.

> We had to make sure the student-
> athletes got a good education.
> We had to balance the budget.
> We had to keep customers
> coming back.

And you know what? I got paid to do what other people pay to do.

How about you? How are you evaluated in your job? Has the performance review process been made clear? I'm talking about the expectations of your supervisor. If not, annual performance review time is a good time to consider this. Do you need role clarification? If you really need role clarification, anytime is a good time to ask.

What are your strengths? What do you enjoy doing most? What is deemed most important by supervision?

Let's take this one step further. *What matters most?* That is one of Stephen Covey's *Seven Habits of Highly Effective People.* It is actually habit number three. It is my favorite. Let's give it a closer look.[36]

Create a draft of your own importance/urgency list or chart that refers to tasks you spend time on. Try to think of examples of tasks that fall into each of the four areas. Where is there the most value for your time? Where do you get the most return?

Covey recommends we spend more time in quadrant number two—the upper right corner—the "not urgent and important" category. Covey pushes us to figure out "what matters most." I have to tell you, I think it is important to have a list of priorities. But don't forget to prioritize your

	URGENT	NOT URGENT
IMPORTANT	I [Crisis [Pressing problems [Firefighting [Major scrap and rework [Deadline-driven projects	II [Prevention [*Production capability* activities [Relationship building [Recognizing new opportunities [Planning [Re-creation
NOT IMPORTANT	III [Interruptions [Some calls [Some mail [Some reports [Some meetings [Popular activities [Some scrap and rework	IV [Trivia [Busywork [Some mail [Some phone calls [Time-wasters [Pleasant activities

Stephen Covey's time management matrix.[37]

priorities. Don't just make a list; make a list and check it twice for importance.

In the athletic world, recruiting has to be a top priority. Remember Pat's dad's advice—you don't take donkeys to the Kentucky Derby. Recruiting five-star athletes, hiring great coaches, and getting the right people in the right spots for your business has be to a top priority. Great players make great coaches, just like the right employees make successful businesses. It's all about the team. Pat always said that she never actually scored a basket. It was all about the players.

Here are some other tools that might help you look at how you are spending your time as well as set priorities:

1. Activity log: Keep a record of tasks. Pay attention to where you are currently spending your time.
2. Time wasters: Identify non-value tasks. Can you identify one or two of your own?
3. Calendar: Make an appointment with yourself (block off time) to work on a certain task without interruption—no phone calls, no meetings, just an appointment with yourself.
4. Action planning: Action plans define who does what and when.

So, now, how are you going to spend the rest of your day? Think about it.

In sports, coaches spend a large amount of their time planning the practices. Pat Summitt always said that her classroom was the practice floor. In planning practices, it is important that coaches keep in mind what their team's needs and priorities are. What does the team need to practice the most? If you observe coaches' practices, you will notice they are extremely detailed, down to the minute. And I guarantee the team with the best practice is going to have the best game.

CUSTOMER SERVICE

Let me ask you a couple of questions now.

Who is your number one customer? *[Hint: It's your boss!]*

Who is most important in the organization?

I had to learn the answer to this one. When I joined the First Tennessee Bank Advisory Board in Knoxville, the first question the bank president asked me was, "Who is most important—the customer, the employee, or the stockholder?" My first thought was that the customer is most important, but I learned from a successful business that happy employees please customers, satisfied customers help the business make money, and in turn the stockholders are pleased. And First Tennessee has been rated as one of the top places to work in this area—especially for women. First Tennessee received *American Banker Magazine*'s award for the Best Bank to Work for in the Country in 2013 and 2014.

Suzy Sutton, my administrative assistant for many years, was key to many, many areas of my life, but especially to three areas—customer service, time management, and keeping my priorities straight. She had the ability to make the customer feel important, while managing my calendar and meetings. Good administrative assistants are hugely important to your success. Thank you, Suzy!

While satisfied employees and customers are very important, it is also important for a good CEO/leader to keep her eye on the financial aspects of the business. I often said as an athletics director that we could win lots of games, but in the end if I did not balance the budget/show a profit, I would probably be looking for another job. Always remember that return on investment is important, too.

At the University of Tennessee I made a special effort to build customer relationships, and it really paid off for me. Here are some very good questions to ask yourself no matter where you work:

> Whose job is customer service?
> Why does your department or job exist?
> Is the customer part of your team?
> Why am I asking you these questions?
> You do know it's all about the people, don't you?

TABLE 1.
Four Seasons the Lady Vols Basketball Fans Have Exceeded
Attendance of the Men's Basketball Fans

SEASON	WOMEN	MEN
1998–99	16,565[a]	15,797
2001–2	14,295	14,230
2003–4	14,403	13,426
2004–5	13,449	12,225

Note: [a]All figures constitute the average attendance per game.
Source: Michael Smith, *Street & Smith's Sport Business Journal*, Feb. 3, 2014.

You may think the answers to these questions are obvious, yet many struggle with these ideas.

There are several categories of customers—internal/external, primary/secondary, direct/indirect. And in my business, there is nothing more important. I have many different customers, too. I have said this before: I often feel like a high school principal in that I have people coming at me from all sides—university administrators, athletes, parents, coaches, fans—you name them, they come to me with concerns.

The Lady Vols built a strong customer base. It did not happen overnight, but it was amazing to watch, and I think it accounts for much of the program's success. Pat Summitt and I went to every speaking engagement that could possibly be arranged to speak about the Lady Vols. We even went to speak to a Boy Scout group one time. Pat's mother-in-law said to us, "You all are amazing. You can even get Boy Scouts to relate to the Lady Vols."

The UT Lady Vols developed a great product, we sold our product, and we let the customers feel that they were

TABLE 2.
Tennessee Women's Basketball Attendance
during the Joan Cronan Era

SEASON	NO OF GAMES	TOTAL ATTENDANCE	AVERAGE ATTENDANCE
1982–83	16	48,530	3,033
1983–84	17	40,046	2,356
1984–85	16	37,450	2,340
1985–86	14	39,282	2,805
1986–87	16	68,852	4,303[a]
1987–88	14	97,972	6,998
1988–89	15	75,939	5,063[a]
1989–90	15	85,234	5,682
1990–91	16	75,811	4,738[a]
1991–92	14	92,942	6,639
1992–93	13	78,025	6,002
1993–94	15	98,137	6,542
1994–95	15	120,477	8,032
1995–96	15	120,624	8,042[a]
1996–97	16	167,992	10,500[a]
1997–98	16	239,511	14,969[a]
1998–99	14	231,915	16,565
1999–2000	15	230,116	15,341
2000–1	15	232,646	15,510
2001–2	14	200,132	14,295
2002–3	16	201,353	12,585
2003–4	14	201,638	14,403
2004–5	15	201,734	13,449
2005–6	14	214,980	15,356
2006–7	16	234,845	14,678[a]
2007–8	15	236,940	15,796[a]
2008–9	15	209,991	13,999
2009–10	17	208,311	12,254
2010–11	17	213,128	12,537
2011–12	15	216,206	14,414
2012–13	18	205,027	11,390

Note: [a]National championship season.
Source: Tennessee Athletics.

important to our success. Just look at the Lady Vol basketball attendance over the years:

In four seasons, the Lady Vols have averaged more attendance per game in a given season than the University of Tennessee men's basketball team. In fact, the Lady Vols ranked third in the SEC among both men's and women's programs.

During my tenure as athletics director, the Lady Vols led the country in women's basketball attendance almost every year. I credit this to developing a great product but also to great customer service.

When I interviewed for the UT athletics director job, President Ed Boling talked about the school's plans for the new basketball arena. It was going to be just for the men's program. This was the plan that the president, the chancellor, and Pat Summitt were all excited about. They had agreed that Stokely Athletic Center (the old basketball arena) would be the exclusive home of the Lady Vols.

I told them if we weren't going to play in the new arena, I did not want to be the athletics director there.

We're saying that we're building one of the finest facilities in the country, and the women aren't going to play in it? I couldn't go along with that.

Fortunately, they agreed, and it was exciting when we sold out the first game. And one of the nicest notes I got from Pat was simply "You were right."

Playing in the new Thompson-Boling Arena from day one gave the Lady Vols both the credibility that I needed for fundraising and political clout. These advantages, in turn, positively affected attendance as well. The Lady Vols have averaged more than 10,000 fans per game since the 1996–97 season, and twelve times they've averaged more than the 12,700 capacity of the old Stokely Athletic Center.

When Candace Parker, the number-one recruit in the country in 2004, came to visit Tennessee, I asked her to tell me why she wanted to come to UT. I thought she might say something about our great university, our tremendous facilities, the beautiful area in which we are located, the great coaching staff, or even the good athletics director at the school—tongue in cheek on the last one. But instead Candace said, "Where else in America would they be scalping tickets for a women's basketball game?" Our customers helped us develop one of the best programs in America. Thank you, Tennessee fans!

Even though you are good at customer service, always ask yourself how can you improve your customer service to be even better—no matter what you do.

> Golf is the closest game to the game we call life. You get bad breaks from good shots; you get good breaks from bad shots—but you have to play the ball where it lies.
> —Bobby Jones

GOLF

I agree with Bobby Jones. I have always said that life is like golf; indeed, I have learned many lessons from playing the game. My current home backs up to the twelfth fairway of a beautiful golf course, and a few broken windows along the way and even a few cries for heavenly support tell me that others learn from golf, too. Here are a few of golf's top life lessons that have had a particular impact on me:

> Show *courtesy* to others; end with a handshake.
> Don't forget to *honor* others; play at an acceptable pace.
> Exercise self-control.

See the end game in your mind; plan your
   next shot.

Instant success is rare; *persistence* is key.
   (See Part 4.)

I was playing golf last summer with a highly competitive Coach Pat Summitt. I told her I was going to out
drive her on the first hole. Wow, did she rise to the oc-
casion! She took my challenge and really ripped one . . .
well, past where I was. That's competitiveness.

Like life, golf is such a mental game, and keeping focus is sometimes really tough. Several years ago, I was
playing golf with Mal Moore, former athletics director
at Alabama, and Steve Hogan, the Executive Director of
the Capital One Bowl. We were playing a hole that was a
fairly sharp "dog-leg" to the left. Steve was younger than
both Mal and I, and he was also a much better golfer. Mal
told Steve that when he was his age, he could hit over the
trees. Steve tried this but hit into the trees, to which Mal
said, "When I was your age, those trees were a lot smaller."

Even if you don't play golf, you have probably enjoyed
watching it on television. Usually, the courses are in the
most beautiful locations you can imagine. That alone in-
spires me.

And another thing—I think sports participation in general and golf in particular offer many positive life lessons
to us as participants.

I can remember playing in a scramble golf tournament
(also known as "best ball") with three pro football players.
I had to figure out my role in that game. How could I help
my team? I was driving from the women's tee. If I really hit

my drive long, sometimes it was the best ball to play from the first shot. That was one way I could help my team. But the *best* way to help my team was on my second shot, to hit the ground to set up a tee for my teammate to hit from. So, I knew my role and I liked to think of myself as a pretty good putter. That was my role. That was my lesson from that game. It worked, and we won the tournament.

Maybe you can think of other life lessons that came to you from golf or from your favorite sport.

As you can tell, I am passionate about golf and continue to play. As the saying goes, you don't stop playing because you get old; you get old because you stop playing.

In life and in tennis,
it is better to serve
than receive!
—Joan Cronan

BETTER TO SERVE

Serving rather than receiving . . .

As women's athletics director, it was always important to me that the Lady Vols gave back to the community. One time, we were all building a Habitat for Humanity House in Knoxville. We were out in the hot sun working very hard. I happened to look up and saw both Coach Pat Summitt and All-American Candace Parker working on the roof of the house. What a horror this was for me. I immediately made an executive decision. I told the Habitat executive director, Kelle Shultz, that they could work on the baseboards but NOT the roof. I mean, I can only give back so much!

Seriously though, I grew up in a family where serving others and giving were very important. I learned this at an early age.

My dad owned a small chain of finance companies in south Louisiana. Every Christmas Eve, we went shopping for needy families who were dad's customers. We would go to the Five and Dime Store—just about the only store in town—right before it closed on December 24, and we would buy all of the toys left in that store. Then we would deliver those toys to the children in the homes of all my dad's customers. To be able to buy and deliver those toys to those children was such a powerful lesson for me, and it still sticks with me today. Every Christmas Eve I try to go shopping for someone in need, just as my dad taught me.

I like to serve both in tennis and in life, and the idea that serving is better than receiving is one of many great life lessons that can be learned from the game of tennis. The importance of follow-through is another lesson, and so are being ready, keeping your eye on the ball, and staying focused. If you have ever played tennis, you have heard these statements.

Tennis is a game that you can play your entire life. There are health benefits as well as social enjoyment, and the friends you make along the way are very special. I still get together several times a year with my South Carolina tennis partners. They are more than tennis partners; they are lifelong pals.

I had the privilege of playing with Betsy McColl, a highly-ranked player and one of my tennis group pals for many years, and we still talk about wanting to win the national eighty-and-over doubles championship in the very distant future. Isn't it nice to have lofty goals? Better start practicing now and working on fundamentals . . .

One year, playing in the Southern Doubles Championships in Atlanta, Betsy and I lost the first set 0–6. The tennis coach in me wanted to change our entire strategy. However, Betsy very calmly said, "I think if we watch the ball and get our sides to the net, we'll be okay." In other words, get back to basics. Guess what? We won 0–6, 6–0, 6–0.

Another lesson of sticking to fundamentals came in a match that Anne Sprouse and I played in a local tournament. We had just recently won the city championship, and we were very confident. We were in a hurry to get the match over and thought we could simply intimidate our opponents. At 0–5 in the first set, we got back to basics. And—whew!—we won 7–5, 6–0.

One more lesson about serving: Minister Bob Gass told the story about Dr. Joseph Parker teaching theology students, "Preach to the suffering and you will never lack a congregation." He told them not to lose their compassionate edge, because they can't heal a broken heart until they can first empathize with it. Hebrews 4:15 says, "We have not a high priest which cannot be touched with the feelings of our infirmities." Dr. Parker said that when you lose touch with people, you lose your touch when it comes to helping them. Jesus went looking for the leper, the loser, the lonely, the lost, and the lowest in society. And He was comfortable around them all.

Serving others is actually good for your health. A survey conducted at forty-four major universities reveals that giving protects your overall health twice as much as an aspirin protects your heart against disease. Dr. Stephen Post, who conducted the survey, says, "Giving is the most potent force on the planet and will protect your whole life."[38] The benefits of compassion to your physical health are so strong that if compassion weren't free, pharmaceutical companies would herald the discovery of a stupendous new drug called "give back" instead of "Prozac."[39]

We serve for different reasons: to get an income tax deduction; to make a good impression and have people think well of us; or because we're put under pressure. You can give without loving, but you can't love without giving. Your time, talent, and treasure are to be shared with others. When you refuse, you're neither happy, holy, nor healthy.

I recall a track athlete who came to us from New York City from a large family. While attending UT, her mother and father were both killed in a street fight. It would have been easy for her to give up and go home, but her way to finish the race was to stay, compete at the highest level, finish her degree in social work, and go back to New York to make a difference in her own neighborhood. Do you know of a better way to serve and give back?

One of my all-time favorite movies is *Pay It Forward*. If you haven't seen it, you must. And, of course, one of my all-time favorite athletes is Peyton Manning, and his foundation is called Peyback. The name reflects Peyton's philosophy of giving back to the community.

One of the things I have had the pleasure of doing with Peyton Manning is serving on the Pat Summitt Foundation Board, of which he is an honorary chair. Our goal is to raise money for Alzheimer's research . . . and to honor Pat.

> Mentoring is a brain to pick,
> an ear to listen, and a push
> in the right direction.
> —John C. Crosby

ONE-ON-ONE

Have you ever been a mentor to someone? I've had that opportunity. Mentoring benefits both the mentor and the mentee. In sports terms, it's kind of like playing man-to-man defense or even going one-on-one.

Let me tell you about a very special opportunity I had to mentor a player when I was Athletics Director at the College of Charleston. I was sitting on the steps of the gym when Nessie Harris came over to talk to me. She was my first All-American basketball player in 1978–79, and it was her fifth year at our school. She had struggled with school—she had not been well prepared for college.

She was having a tough time. I told Nessie that she HAD to graduate.

Nessie said to me, "Even if I graduate, my grades are so bad that I will never get a job."

I told her she had an opportunity to make a difference. She listened. She kept going. She graduated. She went on for her Master's degree. A few years later, she was named teacher of the year in her school. She has also gone on to be a successful administrator for the state of South Carolina. I am extremely proud of her.

Whew!

Doug Kose, a fellow athletics administrator, recently left athletics to become director of Big Brothers and Big Sisters. As we talked about his transition, it was amazing to discover how our work in athletics mirrors the work being done in the Big Brothers and Big Sisters program. We as coaches and administrators often play the role of the big brother/big sister in the lives of young people.

Sometimes, if we take the time to talk with someone—really talk with someone—we have the opportunity to make a difference for them or even to help them make the difference.

What a great opportunity! Don't miss yours . . .

Remember that a mentor can be more than a person. There are so many good books and good movies out there—I am a huge audio books fan. You can also learn a lot simply by watching people and how they react.

Go one-on-one sometime. You can do it. Mentor someone. Help them help themselves. Take the time to help folks and try to visit with them, because I have learned that it's not what you say—it's just about being you. I've had people remark, "I didn't know what to say." But it is less about what you say and more about just being there.

What a pleasure it has been for me to continue my relationship with Nessie Harris and watch her succeed in coaching, teaching, and administration. She is truly making a difference, and I am proud to call her my friend.

Nessie also was very fortunate to have an outstanding coach in Nancy Wilson, long-time coach at the University of South Carolina and the College of Charleston. One of the reasons Nancy was a great mentor was because she spent a lot of one-on-one time with her players. I also think that helped her to be a great coach.

Unity is strength . . . when there
is teamwork and collaboration,
wonderful things can be achieved.
—Mattie Stepane

Teamwork allows common people
to achieve uncommon results.
—Pat Summitt

Offense sells tickets; defense wins games;
and rebounding wins championships.
—Pat Summitt

TEAMWORK

Teamwork.

Have you ever been part of a successful team—in sports, at work, at church, in your neighborhood?

What did your experience feel like—your successful teamwork? Think about it. What made that team a success? What characteristics made your team experience a winner?

Were you part of a special project? Was your team a natural work group that had been together for a while? How many team members were there? Was it a diverse group? Was there a team leader? Who was it?

Take a minute and think about some of your successful team's traits.

Does this team success happen every time out? What makes the difference?

If you can describe your team's success, then you know what a good result looks like. If you know what a good result looks like, you are in a better position to try and recreate those circumstances or that environment.

As I think of the Lady Vols' successful teams over the years, I realize that none of them have been alike. But some of the common ingredients were having the same goal, caring about each other, understanding strengths and weaknesses of each other, and being willing to work hard. With these ingredients, I believe you have the formula of a national championship-caliber team.

The best example I can think of for team unity is the mile relay in track. So many times it is not the fastest individual runners who win but the four who work together best as a team. The importance of the handoff is huge—that transition with the baton, and finishing well, too.

We often hear you are only as strong as your weakest link. Volleyball is the sport in which you can see this most clearly: you cannot hide a weaker player. Coaches are always looking for the weakness so they can take advantage of it and gain the edge in competition.

OPPOSITE: I am very proud to have had the new Volleyball Practice Center at the University of Tennessee named for me. Courtesy UT Photo Services.

I was meeting with a financial advisor not long ago who said that I needed an offensive plan AND a defensive plan with my investments. I had not heard of this before. I first thought I was in the wrong meeting. But the advisor said you need a good offense (e.g., stocks) and a good defense (e.g., annuities or more stable investments). This was his way of describing diversifying in sports terms.

After visiting with the financial advisor I told him about Coach Pat Summitt's plan. Pat said that offense sells tickets, defense wins games, and rebounding wins championships.

She knows about teams.

It's how you deal with failure that
determines how you achieve success.
—David Feherty

Discipline yourself before
someone else does.
—Pat Summitt

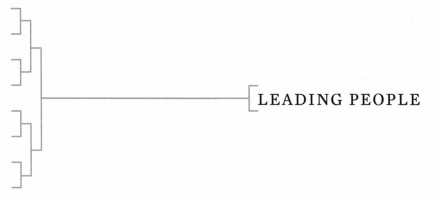 LEADING PEOPLE

People seem to hate performance evaluations, but it ought
to be something we look forward to. Think again if you
will about a sports coach in practice. Think about how
important practice is for sports teams. Athletes receive
performance feedback every day—every practice offers
feedback. Maybe with business, employees need more
ongoing feedback, too.

In sports and in business, we know who the hard
workers and the good performers are on our teams. We
also know how to get everyone on our teams to perform
better—reward their good performance.

It seems to me that managing people is part of being a leader. Guiding and advising either a player or an employee is a crucial part of the leader's job, and leaders must constantly adjust. We are all about continuous improvement that includes improving performance, and if we want to improve, we need feedback, both positive and constructive.

I encourage you to set clear expectations that will enable your people to reach specific performance goals. If you set priorities with the athlete or employee, that should help them be more successful.

American Olympian, Wesleyan track All-American, and author Jeff Galloway teaches about "specificity of training."[40] That is, if you want to run a good 5K time, you have to run a lot of 5K distance workouts. You have to train for that distance—the distance for the event you want to succeed in. It sounds simple, but we do not always do it.

In his book *The Inner Game of Tennis,* Timothy Gallwey suggests that coaching is unlocking people's potential to maximize their own performance.[41] He wanted to remove internal obstacles so that players could be more successful. Chances to coach include motivating, team building, solving problems, and giving performance appraisals (both informal and formal).

If we talk about managing performance, something else that we can talk about in sports is how you manage the game in basketball during the last five minutes. For example, when do you foul? And when do you use your timeouts?

In *Coaching for Performance,* John Whitmore says, "Coaching can occur spontaneously in a minute or an hour-long session."[42] Whitmore also believes it is particularly important to see people in terms of their future potential, not in terms of their past performance.

I have also learned that ongoing feedback—all year long, all career long—can be extremely helpful to job performers as well as sports performers—not just one meeting per year for a performance review or once every now and then for poor performance. Performance review should be constant. When coaching a sports team, I believe it is very important to have an ongoing dialogue with the athlete about her performance. And you know, it's a two-way street. The athlete in turn needs to keep the coach posted on fitness, injuries, questions about plays, and ideas for improving.

Managing performance also means managing yourself. The best golfers have short memories: you have to forget the bad shot and move on. You have to stay focused, because the score on the eighteenth hole is just as important as the one on the first hole.

In business and in sports we all need goals. But to reach those goals, the most important thing is the process. As I have said before, I have told coaches not to think only about the championships, but to remember to enjoy the journey as well. I really think Pat Summitt enjoyed practices as much as or more than games. To win, you have to fall in love with the process. If I want to shoot par, I have to be willing to enjoy working on my short game, my putts, my drive, etc.—the fundamentals.

It's important to focus on improvement. Some questions you may want to ask include:

> How did I do?
> Where do I need help?
> Where am I going?

I think it is important to have meaningful conversations about work and performance. One of the most powerful things I have seen recently was a work group going through their department procedures together. The team was collectively reviewing their work processes mainly as a means of updating the steps, but by going through them together everyone was involved in the discussion about how to do the work. Everyone had input, and everyone learned from the activity. It was truly a great way to handle this task.

Why is it so difficult for some leaders to talk with their teams about performance? Why can't we sit down and talk with another person consistently, all year long as needed about their performance? Why is it especially difficult to have discussions about poor performance? I think one of the reasons we have so much trouble with performance evaluations is because we don't know the people we are evaluating very well. If we know what makes them tick, we are in a better position to advise them and help them.

Remember, the better we know our players and employees, the more comfortable we become with giving them feedback. The water cooler conversations (including retreats, two-a-day practices, etc.) can help you better understand your team.

In your communications it is important that you be direct, succinct, and on target regarding exactly what you want your team members to know and understand. This is a place where flowery language does not help. Our employees need to understand the request.

If we looked at performance evaluation as a way of helping people grow and develop, wouldn't it be easier? Remember that immediate feedback is also important.

Even if all you do is say something like, "How do you think you are doing?" and/or "What can I do to help you?" you could make a difference for the people on your team.

Culture eats strategy
for breakfast every morning.
—Peter Drucker

CULTURE

As you evaluate your processes, let me suggest that it may be even more important to evaluate your work culture—the overall climate of the organization. Are employees generally positive, motivated to work together, free to express feedback, and open to ways to improve? You cannot execute a strategic plan without the right culture. The culture has to support your plan.

What is the culture like where you work? Is it such that it can be defined or labelled? Is it a strong culture? Is it a positive or a negative one?

The Lady Vols tried to have a very supportive culture; we worked to make it warm and inclusive. I always felt that I wanted staff, coaches, and athletes feeling welcome to what we called the Lady Vol family. It goes back to my saying that it is important to remember who you are and who you represent. This is the theme of our culture.

Whatever your culture is, it is significant. Your culture must be recognized and addressed, because culture can overpower (and undermine) new ideas, strategies, and/or approaches that enter the organization from the outside or from other areas.

This is an important consideration for you as a manager or program leader. Knowing your culture and how to communicate within it is important. Knowing how and when to present new ideas is important, too. Say you have a new idea for improving employee motivation—you would like to implement a strategy to help energize the workforce. It is something to which you have given a fair amount of thought, and you are ready to try it. You go for it, but people react in a negative manner, essentially rejecting your idea. Where do you go from there?

It may help to have a communication plan for your culture. It could help you align your message as well as obtain support with key people. You may even want a culture-change plan that could include a champion and stakeholders to help implement a new strategy in a challenging culture. Perhaps it will even be necessary to repeat the message a few times in different forms and fashions to "get it through."

As simple as it sounds, explain carefully what you are proposing. A good logical statement that outlines 1) from, 2) to, and 3) because may help sell your strategy.

There are companies that preserve more of a steady-state environment—a "don't rock the boat"-type culture. A company that has created a more creative culture in which it is okay to question why things are done the way they are or to dare to try something new might not only be more successful but also find that the journey will be more enjoyable.

I have already quoted Jim Collins, the author of the book *Good to Great*, who has also written another book called *Great by Choice*.[43] Collins tells us that businesses have a choice about whether to create an effective culture. I believe we had a choice to create the family culture we developed in the Lady Vol organization.

Your culture is also an indicator of your priorities. I felt like our culture needed to reflect pride and passion in what we did. It needed to reflect our belief that people are important, and our conviction that the "student" in student-athlete was of utmost importance.

One coach will impact more young
people in one year than the average
person does in a lifetime.
—Dr. Billy Graham

God has two dwellings;
one in heaven,
and the other in a meek
and thankful heart.
—Izaak Walton

HEAVEN

When we all get to heaven, St. Peter will be there at the
gate to greet us, and I think he will ask us to show him
our scars. If we say we don't have any, I think he will ask
us if there wasn't anything on earth worth fighting for.

Do you have any scars?

I do.

I have scars from the battles in a man's world to promote women in sports. The weapons used in battle were
persuasion, persistence, and passion—all of which equaled
excellence.

I've got a couple of stories for you on this topic.

And Title IX provided the battlefield where I earned most of my scars. I think Title IX was so important. You know, it's the law that provided equal opportunity in sports and education for men and women. Reasons for my avid support of Title IX can be found in all of the lessons that I am talking about in this book.

Until Title IX women did not have the opportunity to learn these lessons.

I am so pleased that the Lady Vol program was impacted positively by Title IX. And I think the success of our program had a positive impact on others. I am proud that the University of Tennessee supported women before it was cool or before it was required by law.

I get asked frequently if Title IX is working, and my answer is yes. I don't have to do a research study to answer that question; I just have to get on an airplane and introduce myself.

I immediately get two comments:

1. Does Pat Summitt stare at you the way she does in competition?
2. I have a daughter (or granddaughter) who is competing in sports.

The Pat question tells me that, if they know Pat's stare, they know about the success of our programs.

And when moms and dads, grandmoms and granddads want the same opportunity for their daughters and granddaughters that they want for their sons and grandsons, Title IX is working.

That is really what we are all about.

I will have scars when I get to heaven to show St. Peter for this fight.

Minister Bob Gass gives us two stories based on the verse, "Demetrius is well spoken of by everyone—and even by the truth itself" (3 John 12):

1. The first story is about a major cross-country race in Malaysia that covered a seven-mile course. Two hours after the race began there wasn't a runner in sight, so the officials became concerned. When they sent out a car to find the competitors, the officials discovered that all of them were at least six miles away, running in the wrong direction. What happened? The runner leading the pack took a wrong turn at the fifth check-point—and all the others followed.

2. The second story is about a sociology class that conducted a study of two hundred young people from the inner city of Baltimore. It concluded, "Not one of them has a chance." Twenty-five years later a sociology professor did a follow-up study and located 180 of the original 200. Of that number, 176 had become doctors, lawyers, ministers, and successful business people. When he asked each of them how they were able to escape their predicted future, they all pointed to one teacher. The professor found that teacher and asked her what she'd done to make such an impact on her students. She just smiled and said, "I loved them, and they knew it."

Paul writes, "Love never fails" (1 Corinthians 13:8).

John Maxwell says, "During your lifetime you will directly or indirectly influence the lives of at least 10,000 people."[44] The question you need to ask yourself is, "How will I influence them?"

When I believe it, I will see it!
—Dewitt Jones

We don't see things as they are,
we see them as we are.
—Anais Nin

BELIEVING

National Geographic photographer Dewitt Jones said, "As I look through my lenses, nature presents me with an abundance of beauty beyond my wildest imaginings. Over and over again, she seems to be saying, 'Relax. There is more here than you will ever need. When you believe it, you will see it.'"[45]

Some people say, "When I see it, I will believe it." Jones says, "When I believe it, I will see it." It is inside out. I have to believe to see. That is pretty powerful, isn't it?

What if you believe it? Don't you think you will see it? I do.

Doesn't that have a positive feel to it? I just love the concept.

Do you remember Jesus' apostle Thomas?

> A week later his disciples were in the house again and Thomas was with them. Though the doors were locked, Jesus came and stood among them and said, "Peace be with you!" Then he said to Thomas, "Put your finger here; see my hands. Reach out your hand and put it into my side. Stop doubting and be- lieve." Thomas said to him, "My Lord and my God!" Then Jesus told him, "Because you have seen me, you have believed; blessed are those who have not seen and yet have believed." (John 20:26–29)

When I believe it, I will see it. This is true on so many levels. For me it conveys passion; it says I believe I can do it, therefore I will. In my career, I wanted to make a difference. At twelve years old, I had a vision that women could compete at the highest level in sports.

In March 1987, I watched Coach Summitt and her staff work with the team while they were preparing to play in a national championship game the next day. Rather than using drills, they actually WALKED through each play that they were planning to use. Pat had the players visualizing success as they slowly stepped through their plays.

They visualized it. The next day, I watched them win the first of eight national championships and participated in cutting down the nets. This was believing and seeing.

Let me share one of my favorite poems with you. One of the people who had a great influence on my life, and the person who introduced this poem to me, was my high school basketball coach, Anne Hollier. She read it to us before every game. It has become one of my favorites.

THE MAN WHO THINKS HE CAN

If you think you are beaten, you are;
If you think you dare not, you don't.
If you'd like to win, but think you can't
It's almost a cinch you won't.
If you think you'll lose, you've lost,
For out in the world we find
Success being with a fellow's will;
It's all in the state of mind.
If you think you're outclassed, you are:
You've got to think high to rise.
You've got to be sure of yourself before
You can ever win a prize.
Life's battles don't always go
To the stronger or faster man,
But soon or late the man who wins
Is the one who thinks he can.
—Walter D. Wintle

We don't even know how strong we are
until we are forced to bring that hidden
strength forward. In times of tragedy,
of war, of necessity, people do amazing
things. The human capacity for survival
and renewal is awesome.
—Isabel Allende

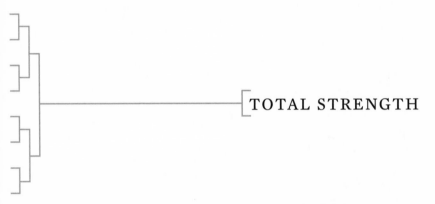

TOTAL STRENGTH

Eleanor Roosevelt said that a strong woman is like a tea
bag—you don't know how strong she is until she gets into
hot water.

We cannot afford to ignore a person's total package.
The perfect performance picture includes self, family,
and work. There will always be stress, but we must allow
recovery time from it—just like the track athlete after a
long workout must allow time for recovery.

I suggest that there be balance for you among the following areas:

Physical. Consider this: Lifting weights breaks down
muscles, but there must be time for recovery. I recently

asked a friend and veteran in the sports administration world, Chris Voeltz, former athletics director at the University of Minnesota, what she would do differently if she could do her career over. She said, "I would learn to take better care of myself, so I could take better care of others." It may be necessary for us to more clearly define work-life boundaries to allow for more physical activity. Our body is a gift from God, and we need to take care of it in many ways.

Emotional. Remember how it feels when you are performing at your best?

Consider this: "The impact of negative emotions on performance is devastating." Berlin native Uta Pippig, three-time women's Boston marathon champion, says, "I cannot run if my body is not happy. I will lengthen or shorten a workout based on how my body feels."

The emotions of winning and losing in athletics prepare us for winning and losing in life. The father of an eight-year-old girl asked me recently, "How can I help my daughter learn to win, but more importantly to lose without going to pieces?" My suggestion was for him to set up competitive settings with him and his daughter where he wins and she wins. She experiences it, and she learns.

Mental. We must learn to alternate periods of stress with periods of renewal. Meditation can serve as a means of mental recovery. Consider this: Training in this area usually enhances focus, time management, and critical thinking skills. This quote from a successful manager underscores the benefits of balancing stress and renewal: "I always take time to sit down in advance in a quiet place and think about what I really want from a meeting beforehand."

I still remember the leadership skills of Merrily Baker, a former athletics director at Michigan State who led the convention for the Association of Intercollegiate Athletics for Women. This was my first national athletics director meeting, and Merrily was so prepared for this leadership role. She led with class and humor as well as efficiency. I remember thinking about what a great presence she had and what a great leader she was. She was prepared for the task.

Spiritual. Affirm what matters most to you in life. Consider this: Energy is often unleashed by tapping into one's deepest values. Pausing more to think and take time out is a good practice, and you can create mental rituals to help do this. Other practices may include journal writing, prayer, or service to others. Visualization can literally reprogram the neural circuitry of the brain. When people feel strong and resilient, they perform better.

I suggest that you draft four goals (physical, emotional, mental, and spiritual) to work toward during the next year. Think about which of your goals is most important to you, and consider several ways to encourage more renewal practices in your life. Here is a sample of two personal goals: In the next year, I will continue to better understand the financial aspects of the world in which we live. Also, I will become a better bridge player to stimulate my thinking and broaden my skills.

Since I am on this subject, I think I need to check on my tee time for tomorrow . . . back to the physical.

In summary here regarding peace of mind, let me suggest you look to financial advisor Dave Ramsey, a University of Tennessee graduate and personal friend of mine. He gives very straightforward advice, which you can discover in his book *Financial Peace Revisited*.

I particularly enjoyed that book, and I have also shared his book *Teaching Kids about Money* with my grandchildren. In fact, my granddaughter, Reese, really took it to heart. One day at Target, she told her brother Quinn, "If you would read Mr. Ramsey's book that Grandy gave us, you would make your allowance go further."

Stay committed to your decisions,
but stay flexible in your approach.
—Tony Robbins

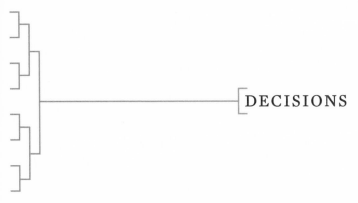

DECISIONS

If you are like me and enjoy being involved—sometimes
in too much—then you need to make choices.

I spoke to our athletes this year about choices and
decisions. They all chose to come to the University of Tennessee, and the decisions they make along the way will
determine their success in life. Often it's the little decisions that make them successful. We can provide them
with everything we can, but they have to make the right
decisions.

I think what the majority of the world doesn't know is
that at Tennessee we have five hundred male and female
students who are not only outstanding athletes but also

outstanding people. Unfortunately, the public only hears about the one percent who make a mistake along the way. I guess what I have learned about our athletes, whether they are my 350-pound lineman or my little diver, who weighs 99 pounds, is that they all have a passion to excel. Our job is to help them be the best they can be.

With the coaches, I think we have created an atmosphere where we care about each other.

Others often ask me, "Joan, do you like football?" And my answer is, "Yes." Football is the engine that drives us. But I also think it's important for our football players to realize that it's critical for other sports to win a national championship, too. We are seeking comprehensive excellence, and the goal is for all of our athletes to achieve at the highest level.

And we create an atmosphere that we call a family.

We have a Fellowship of Christian Athletes (FCA) group. We have an Athletes in Action group. We've created what we call "Team United." We have the best of FCA and the best of Athletes in Action, and they work together. That cohesive sense of family is very important.

I heard the Spelman College (Atlanta) choir perform a song declaring, "I choose to change the world." It was beautiful, and it made me really take pause. I wanted to change the world at twelve years old, and I had the ability to stay focused and passionate about that. I also had the ability to surround myself with the right people—with my "life support" system. This helped me make the right decisions along the way in my career.

Think about what a leader is. To me the best definition was given by Jerry Jones, owner of the Dallas Cowboys. He said, "A leader is a person with a vision and a sphere of influence to make it happen." I think that really tells it all. If I sat behind my desk all day and filled out papers, I wouldn't be a leader. I must have that sphere of influence to make things happen.

In fact, not long ago I heard a young woman speak at an FCA conference. She told us about how she had lived in a homeless shelter during her senior year of high school. Then, with an athletic scholarship, she went to college. Now she works with the FCA staff making a difference in other people's lives.

Of all the decisions you make as a leader, the two most difficult are hiring and firing. I wish I had had the crystal ball that would have always guaranteed the perfect hire. I do think due diligence on the front end helps your success rate, but sometimes it just doesn't work out. The worst mistake is to ignore the situation. This undermines the culture, builds resentment, and kills respect.

Deciding that someone is just not the right fit for your team creates an uncomfortable position for all. Even Mary Poppins's advice ("a spoonful of sugar helps the medicine go down") may not work. The only thing I can think of that helps is your own belief that you have done everything possible to help the people on your team succeed. Sometimes the issue is simply culture, timing, or circumstances beyond everyone's control, but when it is time to make a change, that is your job as a leader.

Below are a few questions for you to think about relating to Part 3—Passion:

1. What is most important to you?
2. Have you taken the time to think about who your customers are and what they want?
3. Have you learned any life lessons from sports?
4. Would you rather serve or receive?
5. Is there someone you can think of who might benefit from you as a mentor?
6. What was your best-ever team experience and why?
7. How do you guide and give advice to people who work with or for you?
8. What is the environment or culture where you live and work?
9. What battle scar(s) have you earned from your career/life?
10. When you believe it, will you see it?

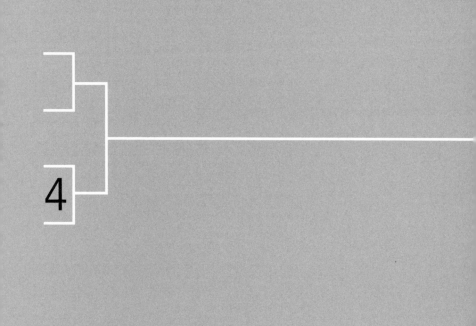

4

PERSISTENCE

I thought I would take us into extra innings—
a few quick hits to help us win the game.

WRITE CLEARLY

A friend of mine who helped me with this book project told me that writing is your second most important skill at work—no matter what you do. My friend said that your degree or specialized training is probably most important—maybe the reason they hired you. But communications—writing, presenting, meeting—help you to become more successful. Writing skills in particular often lead to promotions and career advancement.

This friend also gave me a few writing tips I would like to share.

1. Keep the words in your writing simple. Thoughts that you express more clearly are more powerful. "Utilize" takes a minute to translate. "Use" does not. The best word to convey meaning to your reader is usually not the longest word.

2. We owe it to our readers to write as clearly as possible. Clear writing saves time, and it's not my time—it's yours. So edit your work, and take out unnecessary words.

3. Try not to put two ideas in one sentence. It can make reading difficult. Good writing averages around fifteen words per sentence.

4. The true objective of writing in business is to initiate action as well as to articulate who is responsible.

Communicate your thoughts simply and directly. Those four thoughts alone may help you. It can also help to read what you have written out loud.

Sometimes the hardest part for me is getting started. My friend gave me a hint on that issue, too. Write a letter to a friend. Really. It is like warming up for a workout or a game. Get the words flowing from your brain to your fingers. It also helps to visualize the person or persons you are writing to.

Also, an outline really helps give structure and order to your ideas. So does organizing your material by chronological, simple-to-complex, or most-important-to-least-important.

Sometimes we as coaches and administrators get too verbose. Our game plan needs to be something the team understands easily, so you need to be able to say it so it is understood and remembered. And bear in mind the thirty-second timeout: you don't have much time.

Also, remember the kind words people speak to you in the hallway. "Hi" is one of the shortest words in the dictionary, but it can be one of the most meaningful. Think about some of the words shared in passing in a hallway conversation and how uplifting they can be.

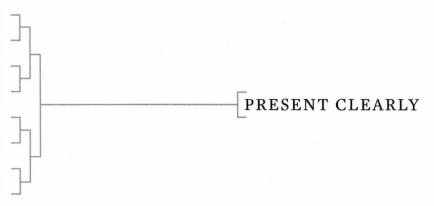

PRESENT CLEARLY

Here are three things that can help your presentations.

> PREPARE—notes, equipment, surroundings, possible questions.
>
> PRACTICE—especially the beginning and ending; how do they sound?
>
> PRESENT—don't forget that most of the time you know your subject better than anyone.

I've been told I am competitive. I don't want to over-play that point, but I do believe presentations are competitions. Usually, it is about getting business, winning support, or persuading people to think or act a certain way. In my line of work, giving a presentation often felt like being on a battlefield where our ideas were accepted or rejected.

When it comes to presentations, O'Toole's Law applies. O'Toole declared that Murphy was an optimist—you know, Murphy, the guy who said if anything can go wrong, it will.

Just a few more points on my presentation about presentations . . .

Know your audience. Especially know your audience if it is a persuasive talk. We must know if they are for us, against us, or don't know yet. We don't want to talk down to them, and we don't want to tell them things they already know. Some people say all talks are persuasive.

Introduction. Should open with a funny story, a video clip, some industry stats, a cartoon, or something suspenseful to capture attention.

Body (70 percent of your time). The rule of three is helpful (for content: introduce, body, conclude; for presentations: prepare, practice, present; for movies: the good, the bad, the ugly).

Conclusion. My advice: Open strong, close stronger, and keep the middle short. People remember most the last thing they are told. Even if all you do is summarize, thank them, and review your key point . . . don't just stop or say "that's it." The first and the last impressions are the most remembered.

One of the places where it is so important to present clearly—to have people understand your passion and the need for what you are doing—is in the fundraising realm. People need to understand exactly why you are asking for support. A good example of this is in the book *Start with Why* by Simon Sinek, a strong reference for speakers. He also wrote *Leaders Eat Last*. Both Sinek books are good reads.

For examples of good speeches, check out the "TED Talks" website. You'll find some master presenters. The book *How to Deliver a TED Talk* by Jeremy Donovan is also a nice reference.

MARKET EFFECTIVELY

Market
Message
Merchandising
Media
Money

The five M's of marketing.

These are five elements of a marketing plan for your business:

1. Who are you trying to reach?
2. What do you want to say to them?
3. How do you enhance your message?

4. Consider the vehicles to send the message;

5. Prepare a budget to make all of this happen.

We have talked about reaching out—and this is reaching out widely.

We have talked about communication—and this is a strategic communication plan.

We have talked about customer service–and this reinforces existing customers and hopefully touches some new ones.

Marketing is fairly easy to comprehend.

But it is challenging to put in place and sustain.

Great marketers not only help bring in sponsorships and dollars, but they also position your product in the right spot. Carol Evans, the Lady Vol's first marketing director, did a wonderful job of what she called the "warm and fuzzy" by positioning our teams such that everyone knew who we were and what we stood for. She was a master at this, and she certainly helped sell sponsorships.

LEAD EFFECTIVELY IN MEETINGS

We have to communicate with staffs, families, community organizations, neighborhood groups, and many other forms of teams. We must work together. We need customer input and direction in all these environments. Some things—actually, many things (believe it or not)—cannot be accomplished by sending out an email. So, we must have a few meetings along the way. How can we guide steady-paced, productive, and effective meetings?

How do we get through meetings without too much pain and suffering?

Here are a few guidelines from my perspective:

1. Be on time.
2. Sit near the leader.
3. Be prepared to share.
4. Talk.
5. Don't talk too much.
6. Listen.
7. Listen more than you talk.
8. Understand.
9. Stay with the agenda.
10. End on time.
11. Include everyone.

Think of a meeting like a team meeting in which sometimes the coach looks like Pat Summitt or Knute Rockne—direct, commanding, and in charge—and other times, the coach needs to put an arm around a team member and let them know she cares. Both are important.

That was pretty concise. That was crisp. Try for that in your meeting. And if all else fails, use my meeting master's guide of things to do: tell a joke, bring food, and leave ahead of schedule. (You can't fail.)

I once heard of a boss who wrote "KMS" at the top of his own agenda for staff meetings. That stood for "Keep Mouth Shut." It was a visible reminder to him, and he said that sometimes he needed to look at that reminder more than he did others.

One of the things that always impressed me about Pat Summitt's coaching style was the time she spent and the importance she placed on one-on-one meetings with her players. She felt that some of the most important ingredients to success consisted of the input given by her team.

We've all heard of the importance of "walking around leadership"—where you are in many places and seen by many. However, that does no good if you don't listen to the people you are trying to lead. This goes back to the book *TouchPoints* and how important it is to know your people. We usually get our best information about problems from within the team.

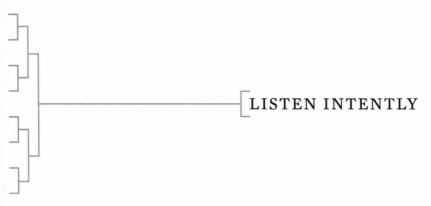

LISTEN INTENTLY

The best listeners reflect what others say. There are five levels of listening:

1. Ignore (low)
2. Pretend
3. Selective
4. Attentive
5. Empathic (high)

Let's focus on numbers four and five—the positive side. Our goal is to be more attentive and empathic when listening to others. It's not easy. I used to do a classroom exercise to emphasize the difficulty of listening. Here is how it went:

First, the students counted off as A's, B's, and C's. Second, I sent the A's out into the hall and said I would join them in a few minutes. Third, I told the B's and C's that the A's were going to tell them a very short story when they returned to the room. I told the B's to act like they were listening but not listen. I told the C's to listen but act like they were not listening. So, each A came back and told a B and a C a story about something simple, like where they went to dinner last night or a movie they saw over the weekend.

The funny thing that happened was the B's found they really did listen more when they acted like they were listening. They found it hard not to listen when acting like they were listening.

Meanwhile, the C's found it tough to listen when they were acting like they were not listening. So, the physical act of active listening—looking at the speaker, nodding your head, eye contact, and gestures—not only tell the speaker you are listening but actually encourage you to do so.

Yogi Berra said, "You can observe a lot by just watching." I would like to add that you can learn and observe a lot by listening, really listening, too. Have you ever tried to listen with your eyes AND your ears? By that I mean read between the lines; see if what is being said matches the non-said or non-verbal message.

That's not easy, but I encourage you to try it. I had a person in my office recently trying to persuade me to support his new idea. He verbally said, "I think these could be the strongest ideas yet for this department." But all of his other cues were monotone and low-energy with very little enthusiasm. This told me today was just another day at the office for him. I did not "buy it" because the words and the delivery did not match up. And fortunately because I listened fairly attentively, I got the whole message to help me make my decision. Really listening has helped me to read into difficult personnel situations as well as make important purchasing choices.

When Senator Howard Baker was chief of staff for President Ronald Reagan, he had lobbyists presenting him with their views all day, every day. Baker was asked by the media if he ever got tired of listening. His response was, "I always listened with the mindset that they might be right."

Leadership knows no boundaries. It comes in all shapes and sizes—education, socio-economic background, race, gender, age—so remember to listen.

5

SIGNIFICANT INFLUENCES

TOM

Tom Cronan was very special.

I know I could not have accomplished all that I did without the support of my late husband.

I get asked a lot about being a female, having children, and putting it all together. Especially in the world I work in, which is definitely a male-dominated world, and a travel-dominated world. I often answer, "It's easy; you just marry the right person." I did that.

Tom was my anchor. Who we are attached to—our anchors—are so very important. As I told my kids, you must surround yourself with the right people.

Tom did a great job of leading from a spiritual standpoint. I miss that. I still remember the day they said he had

Joan and Tom at formal event.

pancreatic cancer. He was the healthiest person I knew, yet he had developed a disease that we couldn't cure, and we knew it. He looked at me and he said, "God didn't give me cancer. But God really cares how we respond." And my answer was, "Well, you'll respond well, but I'm not sure about me."

I don't think we would have made it through Tom's illness without faith.

I was just in New York and rode by *Good Morning America*. I pictured Tom on his motorcycle with Robin Roberts on the back, riding down the streets of New York promoting wellness and research. He rode that Lady Vol motorcycle from Knoxville to Miami to New York to San Francisco for his cause. He spoke to the wellness community at twenty-five centers across the country, and that was his way of giving back and making a difference. It was also a good excuse for him to ride a motorcycle, which he loved.

Together we fought that awful disease, and we did some wonderful things along the way. We have got to find a cure for pancreatic cancer!

John Maxwell, one of my favorite leadership authors, said in a speech to athletics directors in Dallas that people at our age sometimes talk about our bucket lists. Maxwell said we all need a life list—a list of things that we live by every day. One of the things Maxwell had on his life list was the idea that the people who know you best should respect you the most. To me, that was a strong life lesson. That was my feeling toward Tom.

And that is why I think it is so important that we reach out to other people. We share our faith by the way we live.

Tom did that better than anyone else I know. I remember one time he came back from a hike and he was grinning. He talked about how we need to carry our own load and how we need to be sure and help others do that. Some young man on the hike was not carrying his own load. He was letting everyone else do most of the work. Tom said that then some of his co-hikers had put some rocks in this young man's backpack—thus he was carrying more than he needed. I thought that was an interesting way to make a point.

Tom hiked the whole Appalachian Trail—from Georgia to Maine. And my thought was, I don't like myself that much to stay by myself that long. But hiking the Trail was something he really wanted to do from a physical standpoint and a sharing standpoint.

It was important to him to live his life to the fullest.

Someone asked me, "Joan, what's the difference between children and grandchildren?" And I said, "As a grandparent, unlike when you're a parent, grandchildren come and go, and the best is you see both headlights and taillights." They come and go.

When we lost Tom, I realized the grandchildren's memories of him were extremely special. My oldest grandson, Chase, is an outstanding student and athlete. I was so proud when he recently told his track coach that he thought he would like to run the hurdles because his Poppy had run the hurdles at LSU.

Another example is a letter written by grandson Reed several years after Tom's death, showing Reed's respect for him. None of us knew about the letter until his teacher shared it with us.

Reed Bristow
10/4/12

My grandfather, Tom Cronan (Poppy), is the most influential person in my life. He was a courageous, fun, loving grandfather who loved Jesus. He also loved to hike. He was a tall, skinny, tan man with gray hair, and he sometimes grew a beard or a goatee. I chose Poppy because he spent a lot of time with me, helped a lot of charities and people who had cancer or other problems, and he battled cancer very courageously.

Poppy spent a lot of time with my brother and me. When I was with him, he always did a trick where he magically pulled a penny out of my ear. When he did that to me, I would always try to figure out how he did that. I could never figure it out though. Sometimes, I would spend the night at my grandfather's and grandmother's house. When it was time to go to bed, Poppy would always tell me an American Indian tale. I don't really know why he told me an American Indian tale. When Poppy did those things, it made me very happy.

My grandfather helped a lot of people and charities. His favorite charity was the Appalachian Outreach. He did a lot of work at the Appalachian Outreach. The Appalachian Outreach is a charity that gives clothes and toys to people that don't have those things. The charity is in Jefferson City. One time he went on a motorcycle trip across America to raise awareness for the Wellness Community because he knew what it was like to have cancer. At each of his stops, he received some sort of media attention. He went from local stations all the way to *Good Morning America* to tell them what he was doing. Poppy reached out to a lot of people across the country. I think it is amazing that he did all of this stuff.

Poppy battled cancer for a long time with a good attitude. He was very courageous. He helped a lot of people with cancer even though he had it too. His cancer kept going away and then coming back. After a long time of battling cancer, the doctors told him that he would not make it. Even at that point he still kept battling, and then the day came for him to go to heaven. I am very sad that he died, but I know that he is with God in heaven.

I want to be like my grandfather. When I get older, I want to be able to spend time with my family. I want to help charities. I also want to be a courageous man who loves God, and someone who cares about others more than himself. My grandfather was a great person and I love him.

Letter from Reed.

> It is up to us to live up to the legacy
> that was left for us, and to leave
> a legacy that is worthy of our children
> and of future generations.
> —Christine Gregoire

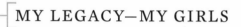

MY LEGACY—MY GIRLS

I am very fortunate to have two daughters—Kristi and Stacey. They are my girls—my loves, my legacy—and the mothers of my five precious grandchildren.

My older daughter, Kristi, called me last night from her home in Charlotte, North Carolina. She was so excited. Kristi said, "Mom! I won a play-off match last night with my local tennis team. We are now going on to the state level. I wanted to call you right away because you understand what it means to go to 'state.'"

That is one benefit of her growing up with an athletics-director mom.

Stacey, my younger daughter by nineteen months, also values our family's sports traditions. "The whole family plays tennis," Stacey says. She even has a tennis court in her backyard where she currently lives.

"We grew up with a tennis racquet in our hand," says Kristi, "and I am very competitive."

I wonder where she gets that.

"Mom and dad gave us words to live by," says Kristi. "'Do unto others' . . . and they practiced it."

I am still amazed that they quote me—and in a good way, too.

They are so different—Kristi and Stacey. One example of their differences was that even though both would do their homework in the car, Stacey did hers on the way home after school, and Kristi did hers on the way back to school the next morning.

"Even with dad's illness, Mom handled things as they came up," says Kristi. "She can see the big picture."

Stacey remembers, "Dad could talk to anyone. He made friends anywhere. We would go to Cracker Barrel after tennis practice, and dad would thank the bus boy for what he did. He was like that."

"When dad was in the hospital, he knew all the nurses and housekeepers' names," she recalls.

"Mom and dad both set an example of showing respect for each other," says Kristi. "Stacey and I married men that made them proud. Mom and dad showed us what a relationship should be. We are so fortunate."

In major decisions that you make in life—and who you will marry is certainly one of those big decisions—there has to be respect for who you are and what you do.

The family gathers at Joan Cronan Day at the Sherri Parker Lee Softball Stadium. I threw the first pitch, and it was a strike. And we won the game, too. The grandchildren, left to right: Reese, Quinn, Larkin (front), Reed, and Chase. The adults, from left to right: Kristi and Rhett Benner, me, Stacey and Kent Bristow. Courtesy UT Photo Services.

"I am so proud of my children," says Kristi. "They are fun little people—my son Quinn is ten, and my daughter Reese is eight."

She is married to Rhett Benner. They live and work in Charlotte.

70 REASONS WE *LOVE* GRANDY

1. She loves unconditionally.
2. She cares for many.
3. She sees more movies than most.
4. According to Reese, she "owns" Tennessee.
5. She gives thoughtful presents.
6. She is proud of us.
7. She can do anything she sets her mind to.
8. She never takes "no" for an answer.
9. She makes the best waffles.
10. She always reminds us to "remember who you are, and who you represent."
11. She's a great golfer.
12. She loves to read.
13. She loved Poppy.
14. She is great at Phase 10 and Catch Phrase.
15. She isn't scared of anything.
16. She is the only person we know in a Zac Brown Band video. (Should be Sweet Grandy, not Sweet Annie!)
17. She reads every street sign and/ or billboard as you drive.
18. She always calls..."just checking in."
19. She works really hard.
20. She always thought girls could do anything boys could do... and she was right before anyone else!
21. She is known for "pullin' a Grandy"... making her own way through an elementary school car line.
22. She is generous.
23. She can put an abnormally large amount of grapes in her mouth at one time.
24. She is a true friend.
25. She values family more than anything.
26. She is the #1 Billy Joel fan... ever.
27. She is a Scrabble champion.
28. She snores louder than anyone else we know.
29. She is kind.
30. She is tough.
31. She is loyal.
32. She has all of the latest gadgets.
33. She bleeds Big Orange.

My 70th birthday card from the family.

34. She is "Pollyanna."
35. She hosts great ESPN slumber parties.
36. She hosts equally great Disney slumber parties.
37. She plans great 10 year old trips.
38. She plans amazing Cronan family vacations.
39. She is good at cooking Cajun meals.
40. She is equally good at ordering all other meals.
41. She is a world traveler.
42. She defines a strong willed woman.
43. She is a leader.
44. She loves to go to Tennessee ball games of all kinds.
45. She is always busy, but never too busy for family and friends.
46. She is a pioneer.
47. She is consistently "fashionably late."
48. She never, ever, ever gossips.
49. She is an encourager.
50. She is highly successful at all she does.
51. She likes to ring her BELLS.
52. She writes great notes.
53. She is quick to tell you how proud she is of you.
54. She reminds us all to keep our "chin up."
55. She has team spirit.
56. She loves to take her Grandkids to all of their sporting events.
57. She is wise.
58. She gives solid advice.
59. She can always be found in a crowd. . . just close your eyes and listen for her.
60. She makes great Smoothies.
61. She is the ultimate delegator.
62. She lives by the Bible verse, "to whom much is given, much is expected."
63. She is full of praise.
64. She is stern.
65. She is proud.
66. She is humble.
67. She is forgiving.
68. She is not afraid to try something new.
69. She is who she is.
70. She is Grandy!!!!

HAPPY 70TH BIRTHDAY! WE LOVE YOU,
Kent, Stacey, Chase, Reed, Larkin, Rhett, Kristi, Quinn and Reese

Stacey and her husband Kent Bristow, senior VP with Team Health, live in Knoxville. They have two sons—Chase, fifteen; Reed, fourteen; and a daughter, Larkin, who is eight.

You want to talk about pride and passion? Let me tell you about my grandkids. Well . . . maybe that is the next book.

"My mom has loved her job," says Stacey. "She has built so many strong friendships in her career. And she maintains those friendships. I think she has a way of really making people feel important."

Athletics is a wonderful platform for making a difference. I have always taken the challenge of being a role model very seriously.

Kristi quotes me again, "Remember who you are and who you represent."

With today's technology, reaching out to others is easier. Use it to your advantage, but don't forget the power of face-to-face interactions. It is kind of like the difference between emailing someone and writing them a personal note: emails are awesome and efficient, but if you are like me, you love getting a note.

I just hope our family can all continue to live our lives through faith. No matter what we do or who we are, we need to live life through faith.

PAT

Wherever I go I am always asked, "How is Pat Summitt doing?"

I don't think I could write a book about sports and the life lessons you learn from sports that did not include Pat and her outstanding career. Pat's life is the best book on leadership that I know. She is an icon for integrity, honesty, and competitiveness. And when Pat was diagnosed with early onset Dementia, Alzheimer's type, I discovered that in addition to being an icon for all of those things, she is also a woman of fierce courage.

Never once in battling this disease has she had a "pity Pat" party. In fact, she recently told me she thought she

After a victory celebration, Pat and I at a UT awards ceremony.
Courtesy UT Photo Services.

would be remembered for winning basketball games, but now she wants to be remembered for making a difference in fighting this disease.

I have three favorite sports books, in this order, that are all about Pat:

1. *Sum It Up,*
2. *Reach for the Summit,* and
3. *Raise the Roof.*

In each of these, Pat and Sally Jenkins wrote so well about Pat's career and philosophy—I cannot add much beyond their writings.

Pat says this about her life: "My memories are not so much made up of information, but rather of episodes and engagements with the people I love. The things I struggle with—times, dates, schedules—are things you could as easily read on a digital watch or a calendar. But people and emotions are engraved in me."

I have found that my greatest passion today is volunteering with the Pat Summitt Foundation and raising money to help with Alzheimer's research.

People often ask me how it felt to be Pat Summitt's boss. My answer is, "We always worked together." Our visions were the same: we wanted to have the best women's athletic program in the country. We wanted to provide an opportunity that was going to help women grow and be successful.

Pat was a great coach. She realized it took great athletes to succeed at the collegiate level. After losing her first game, Pat called home and talked to her dad, hoping to get some encouraging words. Her dad said, "You don't take donkeys to the Kentucky Derby." What did he mean? You have got to go out and recruit.

As athletics director, I always thought part of my job was to help recruit by providing Pat and all the coaches with the tools and the atmosphere that attracted great athletes. That sphere of influence had an impact.

Pat Summitt was a great coach because she was a great teacher. She was a teacher with a passion, and her basketball court was her classroom. The lessons she taught there have made a difference in so many young women's lives—lessons about discipline, hard work, commitment, responsibility, and accountability.

Pat has always been known for that stare seen 'round the world—and for her quotes. According to Sally Jenkins, Pat's three favorite quotes are:

1. "Attitude is a choice." She doesn't just recite this all the time—she lives it. I've never seen her have a bad attitude, about anything, ever. She makes the best of everything.

2. "It is what it is—but it will become what you make of it." Another one she says constantly and also lives. Pat never sugarcoats. How many teams did she ever have that were complete, with no shortcomings in talent or personnel? Only one, and that was the undefeated team. The rest all had major deficits, but she always found a way to make them better. She loved "project teams," fashioning a raw group into contenders.

3. "We keep score in life because it matters. It counts. Too many people opt out, because they're afraid to commit. They're afraid of failure."

FAMILY

As I look at myself and my life, I have to say my mom and dad were the ones who made sure that every time the church doors opened, I was there. I didn't have a choice. I knew that I went to church on Sunday, and I couldn't go to the movies on Sunday afternoon unless I went to church that morning.

I had a mainstay, and I also had parents who said I could do anything I wanted to do. They didn't try to limit what they thought I was capable of. They didn't understand athletics and they weren't athletes, but they knew I had this passion. They were supportive. Even my younger sister and brother, Lera and Charles, were not athletes, but they attended a whole lot of ball games. I think they have learned to appreciate the influence of sports.

I also appreciate Tom's family. Tom's sisters, brother, and their families have also had a tremendous impact on my life. They accepted me as a part of their family immediately and still do. I love my brothers-in-law, or as we call ourselves—the out-laws.

There is not anything we can do that is more important than leading someone down life's walk with us. I believe the example of what we do day in and day out is really more important than what we do on Sunday morning. Sunday mornings are celebrations, and I love that opportunity. But I do think it is what we do every day that is important.

6

CLOSING

WHAT OTHERS SAY

The following notes are highlights from a few of the many interviews conducted for this book.

Compiled By Rob Schriver

Joan Cronan has changed me for the better. We've only known each other two years, yet I've grown to greatly admire her depth of thought and warmth to others in the short time we've worked together. She says to me that there's nothing wrong with taking the high road . . . then she adds quickly, often there is less traffic there, too.

I must show you some of the quotes I have collected about Joan. She is far too modest to share this praise. The messages below are both powerful and on point. What a nice variety of remarks about a remarkable woman! Look at the wonderful comments these people from all parts of her life have provided:

ANNE HOLLIER

"Joan Cronan was a natural-born leader," Coach Anne Hollier (Joan's high school coach at Opelousas, Louisiana) said with her Cajun accent. "She was a ninth grader; we had not had much success up to that point. Joan became the missing piece that led us to a championship."

Hollier saw Joan come in as a freshman and coached her all four years. The coach said that Joan immediately demonstrated observable leadership qualities. "Others gravitated to her. That is not a talent that most have. Even on the forward side, playing three on three (before the women's game went to five on five full-court), the way she presented herself showed charisma."

Hollier also called her young star the "glue" that held the team together. The coach recalled calling a timeout in tough situations and watching how Joan responded. "In the timeout she would be listening and watching carefully, and then at the end she would be the one to say something like . . . okay, let's go do it!"

Hollier said that Joan developed into an outstanding player and that Joan was determined and focused on the task at hand. "She was a strong competitor, too."

They have remained good friends since Joan's high school days.

ANN FURROW

First female student to hold an athletic scholarship at UT (in golf through the men's team) and first female representative to the UT Board of Trustees, Ann Furrow sees Joan from various viewpoints.

"We have been close friends," said Ann Furrow; "I admire her character, her competitiveness, and her compassion."

Furrow also said, "Both of us were young female athletes before it was cool. We had the drive and determination to work for equal opportunity."

"Joan would have been a leader no matter what she did," said Furrow. "She was a woman of character and made us do things right."

SUSAN WILLIAMS

"In terms of expanding the women's athletic department's financial support, I could not have done what I did without Joan's help," said Susan Williams, Senior Associate Athletics Director for Development and UT Board of Trustees member.

"Joan said that she wanted on her tombstone: 'I made a difference.' Well, let me tell you, Joan Cronan has made a difference at UT and at a national level for women's sports," said Williams.

Joan was a unique leader in a unique position, and UT gave her the platform to be successful. She was very skilled at personnel selections, too. She had the right people in key positions.

JOE JOHNSON

One of Joan's former bosses said something similar. UT President Emeritus Joe Johnson said, "Joan has had the unique ability to represent herself, women's athletics, and the entire university well. That's her greatest asset."

You want your leader in athletics to be honest and committed to doing the right things right. With Joan, you never had to worry. According to Johnson, she did not cut corners.

Johnson also said that Joan was a wonderful face for women's athletics. Even at SEC Tournaments, Joan was always the person working the crowd. You would have thought she was running for governor. You don't end up being the chair for the United Way Campaign without being a leader.

KAREN WEEKLY

"She gave me my first chance to be a full-time, division-one head coach," said Karen Weekly, Co-Head Lady Vol Softball Coach. "She provides you with what you need and lets you do your job. She lets her people use the strengths they have."

"At the same time you can go to her with personal player issues. Joan Cronan has always been a sounding board for us," said Weekly, one half of the Lady Vol Softball Coaching leadership with her husband Ralph.

"She was always an asset in recruiting, too," said Weekly. "Joan met with our recruits and talked about what it takes to be a Lady Vol. Joan took Monica Abbott in to meet Pat Summitt on her campus visit. Pat asked her if she was sure she didn't want to play basketball. Joan taught me that with the Lady Vol program, the sum is greater than the parts. She also taught me about making tough decisions in athletics."

ANNE SPROUSE

Anne Sprouse, currently chaplain at UT Hospital, played basketball for Cronan, as well as volleyball and tennis for the UT Lady Vols in the late 1960s. Anne was a superior athlete, although she is modest to point out that teams at that time were more like sports clubs.

Anne said that she learned a lot from playing as a Lady Vol that helped her in life. "I don't think there is any doubt about it," she said. "The team sport is a great lesson. Even in tennis, going from singles to doubles forces you to think about someone else. I can look at things from a team perspective."

Sprouse also said that good competition is healthy. "I'm competitive by nature," she explained. "Competition was a part of my family growing up with my dad and my brothers. Competing with and for Joan in sports enhanced my life."

"We used to have 'jock' days with some of our friends," she continued. "We played three sets of tennis, eighteen holes of golf, shot basketball, and then if we had time we would go bowling. That was a tiring day, and a day that I could not do every day. But we sure had fun."

JANE FLEMING

When Jane Fleming went to The Wharton School at the University of Pennsylvania for an executive training program in business, there were two women in a class of thirty. These were top executives who were being groomed for the top positions in their corporations—serious-minded, smart, aggressive—earning Wharton the nickname "president's school." Fleming said that Tennessee's women had just won several national championships in a row, "so in my introductory remarks that each of us gave to the group, I added (more as a side note at the last minute) that I had been a Lady Vol. Well, I truly had underestimated the response this would get—the men loved it! It seems being a winner and competing at the highest levels is a universally desired asset. It set me apart."

During Fleming's business career, her sports background made it possible for her to enter many inner circles that would have been closed were it not for her athletic abilities, interests, and knowledge.

JIMMY CHEEK

Cronan's most recent boss, UT Chancellor Jimmy Cheek, said, "Joan has so much connectivity with people! She is a motivator. She has a tremendous spirit. She has been a trailblazer. She has had a tremendous dedication to the university as a whole. I admire her especially for promoting women's athletics."

Cheek also said that Joan has been a leader in promoting women's athletics and the university as a whole. He stated, "She always said that athletics is the 'front porch' for the university—athletics is such a visible portion of the university. She has been a very effective spokesperson for UT."

"Her integrity may be the best thing about her. And I also admire the vision she had about what women's athletics needs and what athletics needs to do," added Cheek.

ALEX MILLER

Dr. Alex Miller, Professor in the Haslam College of Business at the University of Tennessee, teaches a workshop of his own in which he talks about lessons from admired leaders. There are only two people that Miller gives as examples in his class discussion about admired leaders: one is a four-star general, and the other is Joan Cronan.

"She demonstrates two strong traits simultaneously," according to Miller's standard for most admired leaders:

1. She consistently gets results that others envy; and
2. She has built relationships that reach far beyond most people.

"As a professor, I really have no particular reason to be devoted to Joan Cronan, but she makes me feel special and rare," said Miller. "She has a boundless energy. I have never seen her tired or complain of being tired. She is always energized and energizing."

Miller also cited as key strengths Cronan's great strategic insights and her ability to converse with anyone from the university president to the person who just emptied her trash.

SUSAN PACKARD

"I will never forget when I first came to Knoxville," recalled Susan Packard. "Joan Cronan reached out to me. She came to make a friendly visit and said, 'If there is anything I can do for you, let me know.' I really appreciated that."

"She carries herself with confidence, which most women could do more of," said Packard. "She has a great sense of humor to defuse situations, especially in dealing with men."

Packard is co-founder and former chief operating officer of HGTV. She speaks of Joan Cronan in her book, *New Rules of the Game: Ten Lessons for Women in the Workplace.*

Susan recounted the story of a little baseball player in south Louisiana. This young girl knew she was good because she'd beaten the boys in her backyard. She asked if she could try out for Little League and was told no. She went on to play other sports. She pursued a career in athletics and became head of all sports at the University of Tennessee.

Packard said that from backyard baseball to big-time college athletics, Joan had no trouble competing. Susan asked "Why are some women comfortable with competition while others are not?" Packard talked about employing lessons from competition to advance careers. Her goal is to help women learn how to unleash their competitive spirit. She calls women like Joan "gamers" and what they are practicing the art of "gamesmanship."

SHERRI LEE

Author and business leader Sherri Lee pointed to Joan as a magnetic and positive force in the community: "People are amazed at what Joan has done at UT. Her personality is amazing. I have loved supporting the Lady Vols."

It was my goal and also my husband, Baxter's, goal to give to the UT woman's softball stadium. We had had success in business and wanted to pick out things around town to give to. We both value education, and I was a teacher. It helped women, and we know that women who compete in sports have a leg up. And Joan was my friend and I wanted to help her.

You know, Joan works so well with people. She is so positive, and you have to be that way in business.

BOB KAPLAN

"Joan Cronan is a very charismatic lady," said Memphis dermatologist Dr. Bob Kaplan. "I have seen her hold a crowd in the palm of her hand."

Kaplan, a UT medical school graduate, pointed out that Joan has been totally dedicated to the women's game. "She has pushed hard for equality in sports. And she has always been upright—always on the up and up. She did what was right."

"You should know that she always surrounded herself with good people—the best she could find. It made her look even better," said Kaplan. "Some people are intimidated to have smart people around them. Not Joan. And I have known her since she came to UT."

Kaplan said that Joan always had the respect of her coaches, and he also said she has great relationships with people. Even her opponents respect her.

"Nobody says a bad word about Joan Cronan!" said Kaplan. "That is for sure!"

Kaplan and his wife Becky have gone to the Women's Final Four with Joan for the last fifteen-plus years. Kaplan, his wife, and Rick and Anna Marie Havens are all big Lady Vol fans. "We love going to Final Fours with Joan," Kaplan remarked.

MICHAEL STRICKLAND

"There are several things for me that I admire about Joan," said business executive Michael Strickland. "I'm a student of leadership. And the two leaders I admire most of all I have seen are Joan Cronan and Pat Summitt."

Strickland said that both Joan and Pat have taught him a lot about leading.

"But the thing most admirable about Joan is her demeanor—she has never spoken ill of anyone," according to Strickland. "She leads people without becoming emotional. I want to be more like her!"

Strickland sees Joan as "grace under pressure." He says that she has in small ways and large ways been important to him – in his business, personal, and civic lives.

"She has this servant-leader philosophy that drives her," he said.

Michael also said that the two finest people he has known as a couple were Joan and Tom—"both so giving; both so caring."

"Tom put you first, always!" says Strickland. "Even the day before he passed . . . I was on the phone with him . . . and Tom was asking what he could do for me."

"And the grace of Joan . . . she is all about everyone else . . . so special . . . I love her."

This photo was taken in the Women's Sports Hall of Fame of which I am President of the Board. Photo by Steven Bridges.

FROM JOAN'S VIEW

Sitting on the front row in Thompson-Bowling Arena behind the Lady Vol basketball team's bench offers a great view.

I can see current President Joe DiPietro, Chancellor Jimmy Cheek just over to my left, and just a little further over, long-time presidents Ed Boling and Joe Johnson.

I can see the cheer team and the pep band just over to my right behind the west-end goal. They are both talented groups and offer lots of athleticism, musical talent, and fun to the games.

I can see the veteran Lady Vol radio announcer Mickey Dearstone and almost hear him calling the play-by-play.

He has a great voice and paints a picture of the game with his words.

I can see the ESPN announcers across the court from Mickey covering the game on national television.

I can see the array of news media and sports information representatives lining both sides of the court as well—coverage from all over the region and nation.

I can see the banners hanging across the top of the arena—eight NCAA championships, seventeen SEC championships, three retired numbers . . . I do have to lean around the jumbotron scoreboard, but it is worth it. It is a neat site. The Boston Celtics don't have anything on the Lady Vols—at least not more banners.

I can see Head Coach Holly Warlick's eyes as she talks to the team during the first media timeout early in the first half. She is focused on giving guidance to the team particularly about getting back on defense in transition against a fast-breaking South Carolina team.

I can see the opposing team—the South Carolina Lady Gamecocks—down to the left side. They are ranked fourth in the country. The level of competition in the SEC sure has risen. They have one of our former players as an assistant coach, too—not unlike several other successful college programs.

I can see the young girls who volunteer to help clean the foul lane during time outs—clean the sweat and dust from the floor for player safety—just one of many projects implemented. My granddaughter Larkin is one of them. Bet she grows up to be a Lady Vol or President of the United States or both.

I see so many concessionaires and ushers that have worked here over the years—some really dedicated souls.

I can see the t-shirt throwers/tossers and pizza carriers also poised in the wings for their timeout promotional activities.

I can see Pat Summitt in her seat behind the media table across the way . . . she has been a regular at the games since she retired. She's still an icon on campus and wherever she goes.

I can see that the upper deck is almost full again. It's exciting to see the fan support.

I can see a section just for our key donors. That is such a good group. They have been behind this program with both moral and financial support.

The sky boxes are up behind me. The people that fill them are amazing.

In my mind's eye, I can see the first team I coached at UT in alumni gym with none of the above.

I can see that things look pretty bright for this program, to which I gave thirty years of my life.

I can see the game pretty well, too.

What a great view it is!

Some really good people. Lots of pride. And hey, quite of bit of passion, too.

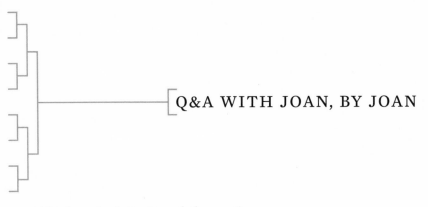

Q&A WITH JOAN, BY JOAN

This is my book. I get to ask the questions.
And answer them, too.

Q. What is the silliest question you were ever asked in an interview?
A. Are you excited about the Lady Vols winning their eighth NCAA basketball title?

I kind of like this. I will take a few more questions
from myself.

Q. Do you think that women and men should make the same pay for the same work?
A. No. Women should make more to make up for the last fifty years.

I may be asking myself questions that are too tough.

Q. Did you ever turn a poor performer around?
A. I can think of one that I am proud of. It was a woman who was having a difficult time in our office. But I got her attention. And she was able to turn it around on her own.

I like these business questions. Let's try another.

Q. How important were processes in your business?
A. Very. That's how we improved. We were always evaluating processes for results.

Q. How do you like to be communicated to?
A. Direct. To the point. Bottom line.

I will keep my questions direct.

Q. What was your vision for the Lady Vols when you started?
A. Building a strong staff and getting more funding to support them.

Fiscal year . . . not physical year . . .

Q. Are you a leader?
A. This is something I work at constantly, and I enjoy the challenge. I love to work with people and watch them succeed.

Sometimes you need to get the lead out to lead— e.g., get out from behind the desk.

Q. Please finish this sentence. In the next year, I will . . .
A. Work even harder than before to make a difference— to do things of significance.

Per author Tom Buford's work cited in this book . . .

Q. What advice would you give to younger supervisors and managers?
A. It's not just what you say, but how you say it. And maybe a follow-up statement, too: there is more to communication than what comes out of your mouth.

Watch those non-verbals.

Q. What is your greatest passion?
A. Right now it's grandchildren. What a blessing!

Times five!

Q. Do you come from a sports-minded family?
A. No, surprisingly not. I was the only one who competed and was involved in sports activities.

But oh, my father taught me about giving back!

Q. What is the most beautiful place you have ever played golf?
A. Augusta National Golf Club in Georgia and Pebble Beach in California.

Okay . . . I know that is two!

Q. Who were your sports idols growing up?
A. British tennis player Margaret Court was always a favorite . . . I liked the way she carried herself. Also, Chris Evert was always such a lady. And Martina Navratilova was such an athlete and example of great fitness. Plus Billie Jean King brought so much to sports—especially for women.

Yes, I am a tennis nut.

Q. What is your favorite quote?
A. "If you are given much, much will be required of you. If much is entrusted to you, much will be expected of you." (Luke 12:48B, The Voice Bible).

Haven't we all been blessed.

ABOUT THE AUTHORS

JOAN CRONAN is a nationally known speaker and business consultant. For nearly thirty years, she was Director of Women's Athletics at the University of Tennessee, Knoxville. She was appointed United Way Chair and Chair of Leadership Knoxville, as well as serving on the First Tennessee Bank Advisory Board, as a Trustee for the U.S. Sports Academy, and on the Board of Trustees at Carson-Newman College. *Sports Business Journal* named her a Champion in Sports Business. She was elected president of both the National Association of College Directors of Athletics and the National Association of Collegiate Women Athletic Administrators. Cronan has been inducted into the

Louisiana State University Hall of Distinction, the College of Charleston Hall of Fame, the Tennessee Sports Hall of Fame, the Knoxville Sports Hall of Fame, and the Fellowship of Christian Athletes' Hall of Champions.

ROB SCHRIVER has been writing about University of Tennessee sports since he was an undergraduate at UT. As a student, he was the sports editor of the campus newspaper, the Daily Beacon, and later started a UT sports magazine, Smokey's Tale. Schriver has spent his career developing training programs at the Aluminum Company of America and the Y-12 National Security Complex. He has written over twenty business training programs on topics such as statistical process control, communication styles, and managing change. He has published in the American Society for Training and Development's Technical Training Magazine, ASTD's Implementing HRD Technology, and Sports Digest Magazine. He also teaches English and communications classes at Pellissippi State Community College and the University of Tennessee, Knoxville.

NOTES

1. John Wooden and Steve Jamison, *Coach Wooden's Leadership Game Plan for Success* (New York: McGraw-Hill, 2009), 29.
2. Peter R. Scholtes, *The Team Handbook, Third Edition* (Madison, Wisconsin: Oriel, Inc., 2003), 29.
3. Vince Lombardi, *Dad's Playbook* (San Francisco: Tom Limbert Chronicle Books, 2012), 53.
4. Jim Collins, *Good to Great, Why Some Companies Make the Leap . . . and Others Don't* (New York: Harper Collins, 2001), 90.
5. Harriet Rifkin, "Invest in People Skills to Boost Bottom Line," *Portland Business Journal*, June 2, 2002, www.bizjournals. com/portland/research/bol-marketing/.
6. Dale B. Carnegie, *How to Win Friends and Influence People* (Gallery Books, 1998), 69.
7. Daniel Goleman, *Emotional Intelligence, Why It Can Matter More Than IQ* (New York: Bantam Dell, 1995), 35.
8. Ibid.
9. James Clear, *Passive Panda Newsletter*, passivepanda.com.
10. www.goodreads.com/quote/tag/actions.
11. Joseph Shrand, *Managing Your Stress* (2012), 36.
12. Stephen R. Covey, *The 7 Habits of Highly Effective People* (New York: Free Press, 1989), 83.
13. Fran Walfish, *The Self-Aware Parent* (New York: Palgrave MacMillan, 2010), 37.
14. Sheryl Sandberg, *Lean In—Women, Work & the Will to Lead* (New York: Random House, 2013).
15. Preston Ni, "10 Keys to Handling Unreasonable and Difficult People," *Psychology Today*, Sept. 2, 2013.
16. Kevin Kruse, "Dealing with Difficult People," *Forbes*, June 25, 2013, Forbes.com.
17. Robert I. Sutton, *The No Asshole Rule, Building a Civilized Workplace & Surviving One That Isn't* (New York: Hachette Book Group, 2007).
18. McMurry, Jane Hight. *Navigating the Lipstick Jungle: Go from Plain Jane to Getting What You Need Want and Deserve!* (Stellar Publishing, 2011.)
19. Larry King with Bill Gilbert, *How to Talk With Anyone, Anytime, Anywhere* (New York: Three Rivers Press, 1994), 53.

20. Tom Peters, *A Passion for Excellence* (London: Profile Books Limited, 2003).

21. Marcus Buckingham, *Now, Discover Your Strengths* (New York: Simon & Schuster, 2001).

22. Martha Duesterhoft, "Coaching Skills," *Training & Development Magazine*, March 2013.

23. Yael Bacharach, "Becoming a Great Workplace Coach," *Inc. Magazine*, Sept. 11, 2013.

24. Ben Mezrich, *The Accidental Billionaires: The Founding of Facebook* (New York: Doubleday, 2009).

25. "If You Keep Your Chin Up," *The Evening Journal*, Pennsylvania, October 1900, Wikipedia.org.

26. W. Timothy Gallwey and Zach Kleiman, *The Inner Game of Tennis* (New York: Random House, 1974).

27. Strosinski, Jean. "Using and Implementing Goals." www.constructivechoices.com.

28. Dale Carnegie, *How to Win Friends and Influence People* (New York: Gallery Books, 1998).

29. Bob Gass, "Word for You Today," thewordfortoday.com, 2014.

30. Ibid.

31. Robert Slater, *Jack Welch and the GE Way* (New York: McGraw-Hill Companies, 1999).

32. Henry Kaiser, Kaiserpermanente.org.

33. Colin Powell, *Business Digest Newsletter*, Fort Washington Investment Advisors, Inc.

34. Robin Green Harris, "Applying the Lessons of the Playing Field to the Boardroom," *insideindianabusiness.com*.

35. Matthew Kelly, *The Rhythm of Life* (New York: Matthew Kelly, 1999), 23.

36. Covey, *7 Habits*, 146–82.

37. Ibid., 151.

38. Stephen Post, "Word for You Today," thewordfortoday.com.

39. Bob Gass, "Word for You Today," thewordfortoday.com.

40. Jeff Galloway, jeffgalloway.com.

41. W. Timothy Gallwey and Zach Kleiman, *The Inner Game of Tennis* (New York: Random House, 1974), 111.

42. John Whitmore, *Coaching for Performance* (Boston: Nicholas Brealey Publishing, 2009).

43. Jim Collins, *Great by Choice* (New York: HarperCollins, 2001), 90.

44. Joel Brown, "50 Inspirational John C. Maxwell Quotes," April 2014, addicted2success.com.

45. Stephen R. Covey, Roger Merrill, and Dewitt Jones, *The Nature of Leadership* (Salt Lake City, Utah: Franklin Covey Company, 1998), 116.

SELECTED BIBLIOGRAPHY

ARTICLES

Bacharach, Yael. "Becoming a Great Workplace Coach." *Inc. Magazine.* Sept. 11, 2013.

Duesterhoft, Martha. "Coaching Skills," *Training & Development Magazine.* March 2013.

Ni, Preston. "10 Keys to Handling Unreasonable and Difficult People." *Psychology Today.* Sept. 2, 2013.

BOOKS

Buford, Bob. *Halftime: Moving from Success to Significance.* Grand Rapids, MI: Zondervan, 2005.

Buckingham, Marcus. *Now, Discover Your Strengths.* New York: Simon & Schuster, 2001.

Carnegie, Dale B. *How to Win Friends and Influence People.* New York: Simon & Schuster, 1998.

Charan, Ram and Noel M. Tichy. *Every Business Is a Growth Business.* New York: Three Rivers Press, 1998.

Christensen, Clayton M. *How Will You Measure Your Life?* New York: Harper Collins, 2012.

Collins, Jim. *Good to Great: Why Some Companies Make the Leap, and Others Don't.* New York: Harper Collins, 2001.

Collins, Jim and Morten T. Hansen. *Great by Choice: Uncertainty, Chaos, and Luck—Why Some Companies Thrive Despite Them All.* New York: Harper Collins, 2011.

Conant, Douglas and Mette Norgaard. *TouchPoints: Creating Powerful Leadership Connections in the Smallest of Moments.* San Francisco: Jossey-Bass, 2011.

Covey, Stephen R., A. Roger Merrill and DeWitt Jones. *The Nature of Leadership.* Salt Lake City: Franklin Covey Company, 1998.

Covey, Stephen. *Seven Habits of Highly Effective People: Powerful Lessons In Personal Change.* New York: Free Press, 1989.

Fletcher, Molly. *The Business of Being Best: Inside the World of Go-Getters and Game Changers.* San Francisco: Jossey-Bass, 2012.

Gallwey, Timothy and Zach Kleima. *The Inner Game of Tennis.* New York: Random House, 1974.

Gladwell, Malcolm. *David & Goliath.* New York: Hachette Book Group, 2013.

Goleman, Daniel. *Emotional Intelligence, Why It Can Matter More Than IQ.* New York: Bantam Dell, 1995.

Gordon, Jon. *The Energy Bus.* Hoboken, NJ: John Wiley & Sons, 2007.

Johnson, Spencer. *Who Moved My Cheese? An Amazing Way to Deal with Change in Your Work and in Your Life.* New York: G.P. Putnam's Sons, 1998.

Kelly, Matthew. *The Rhythm of Life: Living Every Day with Passion and Purpose.* New York: Touchstone, 1999.

King, Larry and Bill Gilbert. *How to Talk With Anyone, Anytime, Anywhere: The Secrets of Good Communication.* New York: Three Rivers Press, 1994.

Loehr, Jim. *The Only Way to Win: How Building Character Drives Achievement and Greater Fulfillment in Business and Life.* New York: Harper Collins, 2012.

Lombardi, Vince. *Dad's Playbook: Wisdom for Father's from the Greatest Coaches of All Time.* San Francisco: Chronicle Books, 2012.

Maslow, Abraham. *Motivation and Personality.* New York: Harper & Row, 1954.

Mezich, Ben. *The Accidental Billionaires: The Founding of Facebook.* New York: Doubleday, 2009.

Moshak, Jenny and Debby Schriver. *Ice 'n' Go: Score in Sports and Life.* Knoxville: University of Tennessee Press, 2013.

Packard, Susan. *New Rules of the Game: Ten Lessons for Women in the Workplace.* Upper Saddle River, NJ: Prentice Hall, 2015.

Peters, Tom. *A Passion for Excellence: The Leadership Difference.* London: Profile Books Limited, 2003.

Rice, Homer. *Leadership Fitness: Developing and Reinforcing Successful, Positive Leaders.* Decatur, GA: Looking Glass Books, 2014.

Sandberg, Sheryl. *Lean In: Women, Work, and the Will to Lead.* New York: Random House, 2013.

Scholtes, Peter. *The Team Handbook, Third Edition.* Madison, WI: Oriel Inc., 2003.

Shrand, Joseph and Leigh Devine. *Manage Your Stress: Overcoming Stress in the Modern World.* New York: St. Martin's Griffin, 2012.

Sinek, Simon. *Leaders Eat Last Deluxe: Why Some Teams Pull Together and Others Don't.* New York: Penguin Group, 2014.

Slater, Robert. *Jack Welch and the GE Way: Management Insights and Leadership Secrets of the Legendary CEO.* New York: McGraw-Hill, 1999.

Sutton, Robert I. *The No Asshole Rule: Building a Civilized Workplace and Surviving One That Isn't.* New York: Hachette Book Group, 2007.

Walfish, Fran. *The Self-Aware Parent: Resolving Conflict and Building a Better Bond with Your Child.* New York: Palgrave Macmillan, 2010.

Whitmore, John. *Coaching for Performance: GROWing Human Potential and Purpose.* Boston: Nicholas Brealey Publishing, 2009.

Wooden, John and Steve Jamison. *Coach Wooden's Leadership Game Plan for Success.* New York: McGraw-Hill, 2009.

ONLINE SOURCES

Clear, James. *Passive Panda Newsletter.* http://jamesclear.com/passive-panda.

Gass, Bob and Debby. "Word For You Today." *Bob Gass Ministries.* https://www.bobgass.com.

Harris, Robin Green. "Applying the Lessons of the Playing Field to the Boardroom." *Inside Indiana Business with Gerry Dick.* www.insideindianabusiness.com.

Kruse, Kevin. "Dealing With Difficult People." *Forbes.* June 25, 2013. http://www.forbes.com/sites/kevinkruse.

Rifkin, Harriet. "Invest in People Skills to Boost Bottom Line." *Portland Business Journal,* June 2, 2002. www.bizjournals.com/portland/stories/2002/06/03/focus6.html.

Smith, Caroline. "Building Self-Confidence: Preparing Yourself for Success!" *Mind Tools: Essential Skills for An Excellent Career.* www.mindtools.com/selfconf.html.

Strosinski, Jean. "Using and Implementing Goals." *Constructive Choices.* www.constructivechoices.com.